英美国语言学校都在教的
英语会话课

| 黄文俞 | 著

北京理工大学出版社
BEIJING INSTITUTE OF TECHNOLOGY PRESS

使用说明

1 《模拟真实情境对话》

每个情境都精心设计了一个模拟真实对话，更能快速融入、身临其境，轻松了解如何建构完整的情境对话。

Additional Vocabulary & Phrases 补充单词 & 短语
- book 预订、预约
  Jane has booked a flight from Thailand to Berlin.
  简已经预订了一张从泰国飞往柏林的机票。
- wake-up call service 叫醒服务
  This hotel offers wake-up call service for 这家饭店为每位房客提供叫醒服务。

★ 随机补充的单词和短语：亮黄底的补充单词和短语，配上生活化的例句，让你一字不漏、学习更完整。

A Welcome to ABC Hotel. How can I help you?
欢迎光临 ABC 酒店。我能为你服务吗？

B I booked a double room online two days ago. I would like to check in now.
两天前，我在网上预订了一间双人房。我现在要登记入住。

A No problem. Let me check your reservation on our website. May I know your name and your Identity Card number?
没问题，让我在网上查一下你的预订。可以告诉我你的名字和身份证号码吗？

A Welcome to ABC Hotel. How can I help you?
欢迎光临 ABC 酒店。我能为你服务吗？

B I booked a double room online two days ago. I would like to check in now.
两天前，我在网上预订了一间双人房。我现在要登记入住。

2 《超高频率使用句》

全书收录超过 500 句的日常会话必备好用句，就是要让你一分钟学一句，快速学习，不怕不够用！

Daily Sentences 高频用句 | 一分钟学一句，不怕不够用

- It's so hot today. I am melting. Let's go eat some ice cream to cool down.
  今天好热，我快融化了。我们去吃一点冰淇淋凉爽一下。
- Do you have any coupons?
  你有优惠券吗？
- Can you recommend me some low-fat ice cream?
  你能推荐一些低脂冰淇淋吗？
- Janet, what is your favorite ice cream?
  珍纳特，你最喜欢什么口味的冰淇淋？
- Does this flavor come in popsicles?
  有这种口味的冰棒吗？
- I want a banana split with chocolate sauce and nuts.
  我要一个加巧克力酱和坚果的香蕉圣代。
- Can I have one scoop of vanilla [1] ice cream in an ice cream cone?
  我可以点一个用蛋卷装的香草冰淇淋球吗？
- Do you want some syrup on the top of your ice cream?
  你的冰淇淋要淋糖浆吗？
- Could we take a look at the menu?
  我们能看一下菜单吗？
- This smells delicious.
  这闻起来好美味。

★ 换个单词说说看 | 用单词丰富句子，让句子更漂亮！

3 《换个单词说说看》

Amy 老师精心设计了举一反三的完美心机学习方块，用单词丰富句子，让你的句子更漂亮，再多的突发状况也不怕！

★ 可依照文内蓝色字旁的星星编号，依照号码对照练习！

★ 换个单词说说看 | 用单词丰富句子，让句子更漂亮！

vanilla [1] 可替换：

marshmallow	wild berry	caramel
棉花糖	野莓	焦糖

Can I have one scoop of _____ ice cream?
我想要一球_____（口味）冰淇淋。

User's Guide

4 《语言学校都会教的超实用日常单词》

Amy 老师在每个情境里，都详细列出国外语言学校都会教的实用日常单词，搭配照片图解，用图片记单词，印象更深刻，不用再怕背的单词用不到，100% 符合情境、100% 超实用！

词性符号说明
- n 名词
- v 动词
- a 形容词
- ad 副词
- ph 短语

5 《Daily Q&A》

Amy 老师贴心设计生活中常见的简易 Q&A，让你学完单词马上能应用在日常的简单对话当中，不再只是死记单词而已！

6 《地道谚语与惯用语》

连学校老师都惊艳的地道谚语与惯用语！课本一定没有教，Amy 老师通通传授给你！有趣又地道的用法，一看就懂，一学就会，让你出其不意地用在日常对话中，绝对让你的口语锦上添花！

7 《7天学习进度表》

Amy 老师特别将语言学校课程设计成"1分钟学1句"，一个时段只要轻松读1~2个单元，只要7天就能用英文行遍全世界！随书附上学习进度表，按表学习，越读越有成就感！

8 《外籍老师亲录 MP3》

全书英文单词、会话完整收录 MP3，同时跟读、矫正发音。就是要让你不用花大钱出国，也能说一口地道流利的英语！

★本书附赠音频为 MP3 格式★

Contents

Chapter 1 | Accommodation & Housing
一天的起点和终点

Unit 1 | Go Home 家 ········ 002
Unit 2 | Go to a Hotel 旅馆 ········ 008

Chapter 2 | Food
大快朵颐

Unit 3 | Go to an Ice Cream Shop 冰淇淋店 ········ 018
Unit 4 | Go to a Bakery 面包店 ········ 024
Unit 5 | Go to a Candy Shop 糖果店 ········ 030
Unit 6 | Go to Burger Queen 快餐店 ········ 036
Unit 7 | Go to a Sea Food Restaurant 海鲜餐厅 ········ 042
Unit 8 | Go to an American Restaurant 美式餐厅 ········ 048
Unit 9 | Go to a Chinese Restaurant 中国餐厅 ········ 054
Unit 10 | Go to a Coffee Shop 咖啡店 ········ 060
Unit 11 | Go to a Convenience Store 便利商店 ········ 066

Chapter 3 | Institutions, School & Work
办正经事的地方

Unit 12 | Go to School 学校 ········ 076

Contents

Unit 13	Go to Work 工作	082
Unit 14	Go to a Hospital 医院	088
Unit 15	Go to the Bank 银行	094
Unit 16	Go to a Post Office 邮局	100

Chapter 4 | Exercising 运动身体好

| Unit 17 | Go to a Gymnasium 健身房 | 110 |
| Unit 18 | Go to a Swimming Pool 游泳池 | 116 |

Chapter 5 | Shopping 逛街好心情

Unit 19	Go to a Clothing Store 服装店	126
Unit 20	Go to a Department Store 百货公司	132
Unit 21	Go to a Night Market 夜市	138

Chapter 6 | Transportation 交通工具畅行无阻

Unit 22	Go to MRT Station 地铁站	148
Unit 23	Go to a Train Station 火车站	154
Unit 24	Go to an Airport 机场	160

Contents

Chapter 7 — Close to Nature 享受大自然

- Unit 25 | Go to a Park 公园 170
- Unit 26 | Go to a Mountain 爬山 176
- Unit 27 | Go to a Farm 农场 182
- Unit 28 | Go to a Beach 海滩 188
- Unit 29 | Go to a Zoo 动物园 194

Chapter 8 — Make-Over 改头换面打扮自己

- Unit 30 | Go to a Cosmetic Store 化妆品店 204
- Unit 31 | Go to a Hair Salon 发廊 210

Chapter 9 — Art Enthusiast 知性文青

- Unit 32 | Go to a Museum 博物馆 220
- Unit 33 | Go to a Stationery Store 文具店 226
- Unit 34 | Go to a Music Store 音像店 232
- Unit 35 | Go to a Bookstore 书店 238

Contents

Chapter 10 — Entertainment
放松娱乐一下

Unit 36 | Go to an Amusement Park 游乐园 ············ 248
Unit 37 | Go to a Movie 看电影 ············ 254
Unit 38 | Go to a KTV 唱 KTV ············ 260

学习进度表

7天学习进度表

每个时段读 1~2 个单元，轻松学习没有负担！
只要 7 天，英文口说就能不一样！

★每完成一个 Unit 请在框框里打勾！

Time / Day	早上 Morning	下午 Afternoon	晚上 Evening
Day 1	Unit 1 □ Unit 2 □	Unit 3 □ Unit 4 □	Unit 5 □ Unit 6 □
Day 2	Unit 7 □ Unit 8 □	Unit 9 □ Unit 10 □	Unit 11 □ Unit 12 □
Day 3	Unit 13 □ Unit 14 □	Unit 15 □ Unit 16 □	Unit 17 □ Unit 18 □
Day 4	Unit 19 □ Unit 20 □	Unit 21 □ Unit 22 □	Unit 23 □ Unit 24 □
Day 5	Unit 25 □ Unit 26 □	Unit 27 □ Unit 28 □	Unit 29 □ Unit 30 □
Day 6	Unit 31 □ Unit 32 □	Unit 33 □ Unit 34 □	Unit 35 □
Day 7	Unit 36 □	Unit 37 □	Unit 38 □ CONGRATULATIONS!

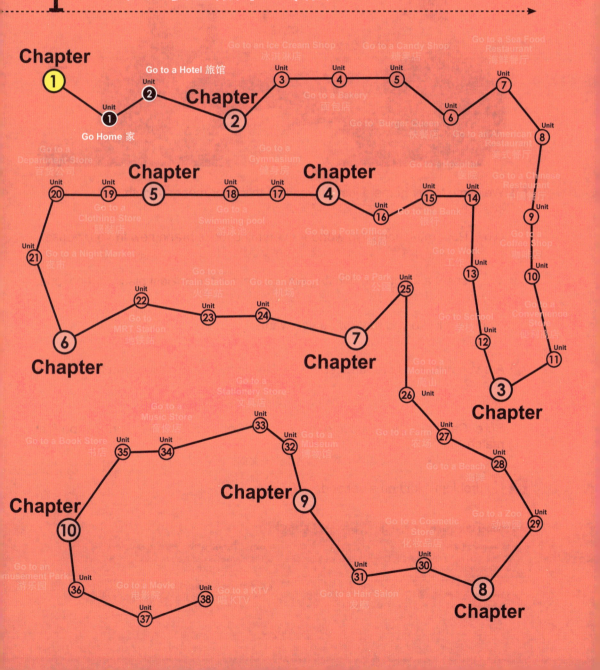

Unit 1 Go Home 家

Daily Conversation | 日常对话 | 模拟真实的日常对话

01-01

A Welcome to my home. I just moved into this apartment a month ago.
欢迎来我家。我一个月前才刚搬进这套公寓。

B Wow. Congratulations. <mark>No wonder</mark> everything looks <mark>brand new</mark> in your house.
哇，恭喜！难怪你的房子里所有的东西看起来都很新。

A Yes. I spent a lot of time thinking how to make it the <mark>coziest</mark> place in the world.
是的，我花了很多时间想如何让它变成世界上最温馨的地方。

B It does look like you have what you want.
你看起来真的拥有你想要的。

A Are you hungry? I prepared some cookies in the oven. Would you like to have some?
你饿了吗？我准备了一些饼干在烤箱里。你想吃一些吗？

B Sure. Can I also have a cup of hot coffee? Coffee and cookies are the <mark>perfect match</mark>.
当然，我可以来一杯热咖啡吗？咖啡和饼干是完美的搭配。

A No problem. Hold on a second.
没问题，等一下。

Additional Vocabulary & Phrases | 补充单词 & 短语

- **no wonder** [ph] 难怪
  Carrie had a terrible cold last week. No wonder she didn't come to our party.
  卡丽上星期得了重感冒，难怪她没有来我们的派对。

- **brand new** [ph] 全新、崭新的
  My parents moved into a brand new house last week.
  我的父母上星期搬进了一套全新的房子。

- **cozy** [a] 舒适的、惬意的、舒服的 (cozy–cozier–coziest)
  The blanket is warm and cozy.
  毯子盖起来又温暖又舒服。

- **perfect match** [ph] 完美组合
  Do you think John and Lily are perfect match?
  你觉得约翰和莉莉是完美组合吗？

Daily Sentences 高频用句 | 一分钟学一句，不怕不够用

- I still need to buy a new **washing machine** *¹.
  我还需要买一台新的洗衣机。

- I love big living rooms. I think a living room is a place where you can enjoy your time with friends and family.
  我喜欢大客厅。我认为客厅是你可以和朋友、家人一起享受时光的地方。

- Lying casually on the sofa and watching TV with friends and family are the most enjoyable things after finishing a tiring day.
  轻松地倒在沙发上和朋友、家人一起看电视，是结束劳累的一天后最享受的事。

- I love watching some DVDs on my bed. 我喜欢在床上看一些 DVD。

- LCD TVs are much cheaper than Plasma TVs.
  液晶电视比等离子电视便宜很多。

- We ran out of **light bulbs** *². Can you run errands to buy them?
  我们的灯泡用完了，你可以替我跑腿买新的吗？

- Don't be like a couch potato sitting on the sofa and doing nothing but eating and watching TV. 不要像一个沙发马铃薯一样坐在沙发上什么都不做，只是吃和看电视。

- The refrigerator is empty. Let's go to the supermarket to do some grocery shopping. 冰箱空了，我们去超市买一些食物吧。

- You can wash your dishes in a dishwasher. What you need to do is turning on the machine, putting some detergent in and pressing the start button.
  你可以用洗碗机洗碗，你需要做的就是打开机器，放一些洗洁剂和按下开始键就可以了。

★ 换个单词说说看 | 用单词丰富句子，让句子更漂亮！

washing machine *¹ 可以替换：
- dryer 烘干机
- air conditioner 空调
- dish washer 洗碗机

I still need to buy a new _____.
我还需要买一台新的_____。

light bulbs *² 可以替换：
- toilet paper 卫生纸
- shampoo 洗发水
- garbage bag 垃圾袋

We ran out of _____.
我们_____用完了。

Additional Vocabulary & Phrases | 补充单词 & 短语

- **casually** [ad] 轻松地、偶然地
  Mom and dad walked casually along the beach.
  爸妈沿着海岸轻松地散步。

- **run errands** [ph] 跑腿、为某人办事
  Cindy ran errands for the boss.
  辛迪替老板跑腿去了。

- **detergent** [n] 洗洁剂
  I need to buy some detergent.
  我得买些洗洁剂。

- **press** [v] 按、压
  You need to press this button to start the computer.
  电脑开机你得按这个按钮。

Daily Vocabulary 语言学校都会教的实用日常单词

1 living room 客厅

television [ˈtelɪvɪʒn] [n]	电视
sofa [ˈsəʊfə] [n]	沙发
chair [tʃeə] [n]	椅子
table [ˈteɪbl] [n]	桌子
window [ˈwɪndəʊ] [n]	窗户
light [laɪt] [n]	灯

2 bedroom 卧室、寝室

single bed [ph]	单人床
double bed [ph]	双人床
blanket [ˈblæŋkɪt] [n]	毯子
pillow [ˈpɪləʊ] [n]	枕头
sheet [ʃiːt] [n]	床单
dressing table [ph]	梳妆台
bedside lamp [ph]	床头灯

3 bathroom 浴室

toilet [ˈtɔɪlət] [n] / restroom [n]	（有冲洗式马桶的）厕所；洗手间；盥洗室
bathtub [ˈbɑːθtʌb] [n]	浴缸
shower nozzle [ph]	莲蓬头
mirror [ˈmɪrə] [n]	镜子
toilet [ˈtɔɪlət] [n]	马桶
faucet [ˈfɔːsɪt] [n]	水龙头
sink [sɪŋk] [n]	洗手台

④ kitchen 厨房

stove [stəʊv] n		煤气炉
refrigerator [rɪˈfrɪdʒəreɪtə] n		冰箱
oven [ˈʌvn] n		烤箱
cooker [ˈkʊkə] n		炊具；烹饪器具
turner [ˈtɜːnə] n		锅铲
pan [pæn] n		平底锅
pot [pɒt] n		锅、罐、壶
chopping board		砧板
hot water dispenser ph		热水机
toaster [ˈtəʊstə] n		烤面包机
microwave [ˈmaɪkrəweɪv] n		微波炉

⑤ housewares 家庭用品

bowl [bəʊl] n	碗
chopsticks [ˈtʃɒpstɪks] n	筷子
spoon [spuːn] n	汤匙
cup [kʌp] n	杯子
dish [dɪʃ] n / **plate** [pleɪt] n	盘子
kettle [ˈketl] n	水壶

⑥ storage 储藏室

broom [bruːm] n	扫把
dustpan [ˈdʌstpæn] n	簸箕
lawnmower [ˈlɔːnməʊə] n	割草机
mop [mɒp] n	拖把
trash can ph	垃圾桶
vacuum cleaner ph	吸尘器

7 yard 院子

barbecue [ˈbɑːbɪkjuː] [n]	烤肉架
doghouse [ˈdɒghaʊs] [n]	狗屋
fence [fens] [n]	栅栏
garden [ˈgɑːdn] [n]	花园
greenhouse [ˈgriːnhaʊs] [n]	温室
patio [ˈpætiəʊ] [n]	露台

8 library 图书室

lamp [læmp] [n]	台灯	**ceiling** [ˈsiːlɪŋ] [n]	天花板
carpet [ˈkɑːpɪt] [n]	地毯	**doorknob** [ˈdɔːnɒb] [n]	门把手
fireplace [ˈfaɪəpleɪs] [n]	壁炉	**recreation room** [ph]	游戏室
bookshelf [ˈbʊkʃelf] [n]	书柜	**light switch** [ph]	电灯开关
blinds [blaɪndz] [n]	百叶窗	**floor mat** [ph]	地垫

Daily Q&A

〔会话一〕

Q ▸ Do you use microwave to cook food?
你会用微波炉做饭吗?

A ▸ Yes, I usually use it to heat some food.
会,我通常用它来热饭。

〔会话二〕

Q ▸ How many bedrooms do you have?
你有几间卧室啊?

A ▸ There are three bedrooms.
总共三间。

〔会话三〕

Q ▸ Where do you put your earrings?
你把耳环放在哪里了?

A ▸ I think I put them on the dressing table.
我想我把它们放在化妆台上。

Proverbs & Idioms 地道谚语与惯用语 | 让句子锦上添花

be home and dry 成功地完成某事
I've just got one more report to finish and I will be home and dry.
我还有一个报告要完成。我会完成它的。

make oneself at home 别客气当作在自己家一样
Welcome to my home. Please make yourself at home.
欢迎来到我家。把这当成自己家一样吧。

hit a home run 在某方面成功
Our performance last night was the best we had ever given. We felt our group hit a home run.
昨晚的表演是我们目前为止最好的表演。我觉得我们团是成功的。

until the cows come home 花很长的时间
We can talk about the problem until the cows come home but it still wouldn't solve anything.
我们可以花很长的时间讨论那个问题，但是那没有帮助。

home is where the heart is 心在哪里家就在哪里
I don't mind traveling around all the time because home is where the heart is.
我不介意到处旅行，因为心在哪里家就在哪里。

the longest way round is the shortest way home 欲速则不达
You had better read the instructions before trying to use your new cellphone. It may take some time, but the longest way round is the shortest way home.
你最好在你使用新手机前先阅读说明书。这可能会花你一些时间，但是欲速则不达。

Charity begins at home. 行善始于近亲
If you really want to make the world a better place, you can start by being kind to your family and friends. Charity begins at home.
如果你真的想要让世界变成更好的地方，那么你可以先从善待你的家人和朋友开始。行善始于近亲。

East or west, home is best. 天涯海角，自家最好。
You may think that traveling all the time is fun, but eventually you'll discover that east or west, home is best.
你可能觉得旅行很有趣，但是最终你会发现天涯海角，自家最好。

Unit 2 Go to a Hotel 旅馆

Daily Conversation 日常对话 | 模拟真实的日常对话

A Welcome to ABC Hotel. How can I help you?
欢迎光临 ABC 酒店。我能为你服务吗？

B I **booked** a double room online two days ago. I would like to check in now.
两天前，我在网上预订了一间双人房。我现在要登记入住。

A No problem. Let me check your reservation on our website. May I know your name and your Identity Card number?
没问题，让我在网上查一下你的预订。可以告诉我你的名字和身份证号码吗？

B Sure. It's Jeremy Pitt, F983412324.
当然，我的名字是皮特•杰若米，F983412324.

A Yes. I saw your reservation. Here is your room key and your room is 709. It's on the 7th floor next to the stairs.
是的，我看到你的预订了。这是你的钥匙，你的房间在 709，在七楼的楼梯旁。

B By the way, I would like to have the **wake-up call service**. I will have to get up early in the morning to attend a very important meeting tomorrow.
顺带说一下，我想要叫醒服务。我明天需要一早起床参加一个非常重要的会议。

A No problem. What time do you want to wake up tomorrow?
没问题。你明天想要几点起床？

B 6 o'clock. Thank you very much! 六点。非常谢谢你！

Additional Vocabulary & Phrases | 补充单词 & 短语

- **book** [v] 预订、预约
  Jane has booked a flight from Thailand to Berlin.
  简已经预订了一张从泰国飞往柏林的机票。

- **wake-up call service** [ph] 叫醒服务
  This hotel offers wake-up call service for every customer.
  这间饭店为每位房客提供叫醒服务。

Daily Sentences 高频用句 | 一分钟学一句，不怕不够用 MP3 01-05

- You can go to our hotel website and make room reservations on the Internet.
  你可以上我们酒店的网站订房间。

- Is there any vending machine on this floor?
  这一楼有售卖机吗？

- Can we have a floor map of this hotel?
  可以给我一张这家酒店的平面图吗？

- Can you hire a taxi for me? I need to go to the airport by 4 o'clock in the morning.
  可以请你帮我叫出租车吗？早上四点前我要到机场。

- What time do I need to check out of the hotel?
  我几点必须退房？

- Would you like to ask a porter to carry your luggage to your room?
  你想请行李员把你的行李拿到房间吗？

- Excuse me. There is something wrong with my room. The hairdryer*1 keeps making funny noises.
  不好意思，我的房间有些问题。吹风机一直发出奇怪的声音。

- The sink in the bathroom is clogged.
  淋浴间的洗手台塞住了。

- We should put some tip on the table in the morning if we need to stay here for two nights.
  如果我们要在这里待上两夜的话，早上我们要放一些小费在桌上。

- This hotel offers some free maps with some discount vouchers.
  这间饭店提供一些免费的、含有折扣券的地图。

★ 换个单词说说看 | 用单词丰富句子，让句子更漂亮！

hairdryer*1 可替换：

| television | air conditioner | toilet |
| 电视 | 冷气 | 马桶 |

The _____ keeps making funny noise.
_____ 一直发出怪声音。

Additional Vocabulary & Phrases | 补充单词 & 短语

- **porter** n 行李员、服务员
  You can give your luggage to the porter.
  你可以把你的行李拿给行李员。

- **sink** n 洗手台、水槽
  Can you clean the sink, please?
  可以麻烦你清理一下洗手台吗？

- **clog** v 堵塞、塞满
  The tourists clogged the road into the amusement park.
  去往游乐园的路被游客堵满了。

- **discount voucher** ph 折价券
  You can pay this item with the discount voucher.
  你可以用折价券买这种商品。

Daily Vocabulary 语言学校都会教的实用日常单词
01-06

① lobby 大厅

enquire [ɪn'kwaɪə] v	咨询
introduce [ˌɪntrə'djuːs] v	介绍
baggage ['bægɪdʒ] n	行李
wait [weɪt] v	等待
arrange [ə'reɪndʒ] v	安排
guard [gɑːd] n	守卫
check in ph	入住登记、报到
check out ph	结账离开、退房

② supply 供给

toothbrush ['tuːθbrʌʃ] n	牙刷
toothpaste ['tuːθpeɪst] n	牙膏
towel ['taʊəl] n	毛巾
bathing kit ph	沐浴用品
bath robe ph	浴袍

③ features 特色

furniture ['fɜːnɪtʃə] n	家具	bathroom ['bɑːθruːm] n	淋浴间
safe [seɪf] n	保险箱	minibar ['mɪnɪbɑː] n	小酒柜
air conditioner ph	空调		

④ facility 设施

banquet hall [ph]	宴会厅
conference room [ph]	会议室
gymnasium [dʒɪmˈneɪziəm] [n]	健身房
parking lot [ph]	停车场
restaurant [ˈrestrɒnt] [n]	餐厅
pub [pʌb] [n]	酒吧

⑤ room service 客房服务

tip [tɪp] [n]	小费
laundry service [ph]	洗衣服务
housekeeper [ˈhaʊskiːpə]	客房服务员
doorman [ˈdɔːmən] [n]	门厅侍者、门卫
bellboy [ˈbelbɔɪ] [n]	行李员

⑥ accommodation 住宿

hotel [həʊˈtel] [n]	酒店
B&B (bed & breakfast) [ph]	民宿
guesthouse [ˈgesthaʊs] [n]	小型家庭旅馆
hostel [ˈhɒstl] [n]	青年旅社
campsite [ˈkæmpsaɪt] [n]	露营地

7 guest room 客房

single room [ph]	单人间
double room [ph]	大床房
twin room [ph]	双人间
triple room [ph]	三人间
suite [swiːt] [n]	套房

8 gift shop 礼品店

souvenir [ˌsuːvəˈnɪə] [n]	纪念品	vending machine [ph]	售卖机
money exchange [ph]	兑币处	information desk [ph]	询问处
newsstand [ˈnjuːzstænd] [n]	报摊	brochure [ˈbrəʊʃə] [n]	小册子

Daily Q&A

〔会话一〕

Q ► What kinds of rooms does this hotel have?
这家旅馆有什么样的房间？

A ► We have single rooms, double rooms and suite.
有单人间、双人间和套房。

〔会话二〕

Q ► Where is the elevator?
电梯在哪里？

A ► It is in the middle of the lobby.
在大厅的中间。

〔会话三〕

Q ► Excuse me. The TV is broken. It just won't turn on.
不好意思，电视坏了，它没有办法打开。

A ► OK. I will ask someone to check the problem.
好，我会请人去查看问题。

Proverbs & Idioms 地道谚语与惯用语 | 让句子锦上添花

be part of the furniture 如同家具一般，固定班底
I have been working for this company for so long, and now I am part of the furniture.
我在这家公司已经工作很久了，我现在已经是公司的一部分。

a rubber check 空头支票
The woman was accused of writing more than 10,000 dollars in rubber checks to pay for expensive jewelry.
那个女人被控告开了一万元的空头支票购买昂贵的珠宝。

some elbow room 再多一些空间
The room is so crowded. We all need some elbow room.
这间房间很挤，我们需要再多一些空间。

don't let it out of this room 不能将事情说出去
This is a top secret. Don't let it out of this room.
这是最高机密，千万不要说出去。

not enough room to swing a cat 空间很小，没有转身的余地
Their living room is very small. There is not enough room to swing a cat.
他们的客厅很小，没有转身的余地。

lobby for something 游说通过议案
The manufacturers lobbied for tax relief.
制造商们游说通过减税议案。

lobby against something 游说反对议案通过
They lobbied against the tax increase.
他们游说反对增加税收的议案。

make a reservation 预约、预订
I made a reservation for a flight at twelve .
我预订中午12点的飞机。

travel broadens the mind 旅行令视野变得更广
It's rather true that travel broadens the mind. You will learn to see things from different perspectives.
旅行让视野变得更广这个说法很对。你会学习从不同的角度看事情。

Everyday Sentences 语言学校独家传授的必备好句子

- Can I make my reservation on the Internet?
  我可以在网上订房吗?

- There is something fragile in my hand carry. Can you ask the porter to be more careful?
  我的手提行李中有易碎物品。你可以告诉行李员小心一点吗?

- Just go to our hotel website. Find the icon for hotel reservation and complete the form.
  只要到我们酒店的网站,找到预订酒店的图标,然后填完表格就可以了。

- Is there still anything I can help you?
  还有什么事我可以服务吗?

- After I put all my luggage in my room, I would like to walk around here. Do you offer any free map?
  我把行李放到房间后,我想要在附近走走。你们提供免费的地图吗?

- Can you recommend me a good restaurant near here?
  你可以推荐给我一家附近不错的餐厅吗?

- You can try our Japanese sushi bar in our gourmet street in the basement. A lot of our customers like it.
  你可以试试地下美食街的日本寿司,很多客人都喜欢。

- Our bartender can make all kinds of cocktails. They all taste great.
  我们的酒保可以调出各种鸡尾酒,它们尝起来都很棒。

- We're out of coffee. How about some milk instead?
  我们没咖啡了,改喝牛奶好吗?

- Taking a shower will help me wake up.
  去冲个澡可以让我清醒一点。

MEMO

From AM-PM 从早到晚都用得到的必备好句子

- I'll call a taxi to pick us up.
  我叫出租车来载我们。

- Could you drive a bit faster? I'm in a rush.
  能请你开快一点吗？我赶时间。

- How fresh are these fish?
  这些鱼有多新鲜？

- I ride the bus to work every morning.
  我每天坐公交车上班。

- I need to catch the bus.
  我得赶公交车。

- Where can I take Bus 287?
  我在哪可以搭到 287 公交车？

- I ride my bicycle to school every day.
  我每天骑自行车上学。

- This is my stop.
  我到站了。

- Where's the nearest subway station?
  最近的地铁站在哪？

- Where can I buy a subway token?
  我要在哪买地铁票？

- What do you recommend?
  你有什么建议呢？

MEMO

- What is today's special?
  今日的特餐是什么？

- What is the soup of the day?
  今天的浓汤是什么？

- Which subway line should we take?
  我们要乘坐哪一条地铁啊？

- This smells delicious.
  这闻起来好美味。

- No sugar, please.
  不要糖，谢谢。

- I don't drink coffee. What other drinks do you have?
  我不喝咖啡。你们有其他饮料吗？

- Do you serve any dessert here?
  你们这有甜点吗？

- Do you have wireless Internet in this coffee shop?
  这家咖啡店可以无线上网吗？

- I'm going to the coffee shop to read and drink coffee.
  我要去咖啡店看书喝咖啡。

- This coffee is too bitter. Could I have more sugar, please?
  这咖啡好苦。可以再帮我加一些糖吗？

- I want some whipped cream on top of my cappuccino.
  我的卡布奇诺要加鲜奶油。

MEMO

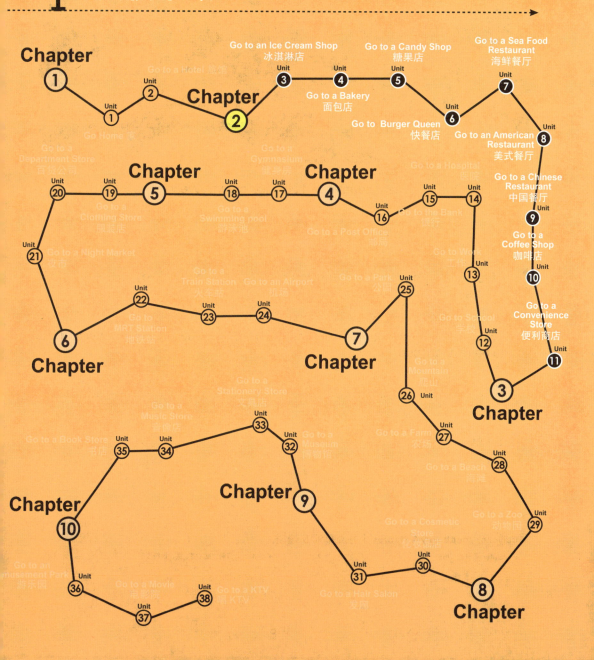

Unit 3 Go to an Ice Cream Shop 冰淇淋店

Daily Conversation | 日常对话 | 模拟真实的日常对话

A Look at the ice cream counter. Isn't the ice cream lovely?
你看那冰淇淋柜，那些冰淇淋是不是很美味？

B It is. I can't wait to have it.
是呀，我等不及吃它们了。

A I feel like eating Swiss chocolate and rum and raisin. They are my favorite flavors.
我想吃瑞士巧克力和朗姆葡萄，它们是我最爱吃的口味。

B I would like to have vanilla and mango with some nuts on the top. I would like to have it in a cup.
我想要香草和杧果口味的，要加坚果配料。我要用杯装的。

A Do you want to order another blueberry sorbet with me? We can share.
你想和我再点一杯蓝莓冰沙吗？我们可以一起喝。

B Sure!
好啊！

Additional Vocabulary & Phrases | 补充单词 & 短语

- **counter** [n] 长柜、柜台
  You can pay your items at the counter over there.
  你可以在那边的柜台结账。

- **order** [v] 订购、点（餐、菜、饮料等）
  I would like to order two hamburgers, please.
  我想要点两份汉堡。

Daily Sentences 高频用句 | 一分钟学一句，不怕不够用

- It's so hot today. I am **melting**. Let's go eat some ice cream to cool down.
  今天好热，我快融化了。我们去吃一点冰淇淋凉爽一下。

- Do you have any **coupons**?
  你有优惠券吗？

- Can you recommend me some low-fat ice cream?
  你能推荐一些低脂冰淇淋吗？

- Janet, what is your favorite ice cream?
  珍纳特，你最喜欢什么口味的冰淇淋？

- Does this flavor come in popsicles?
  有这种口味的冰棒吗？

- I want a banana split with chocolate sauce and nuts.
  我要一个加巧克力酱和坚果的香蕉圣代。

- Can I have one scoop of **vanilla***¹ ice cream in an ice cream cone?
  我可以点一个用蛋卷装的香草冰淇淋球吗？

- Do you want some syrup on the top of your ice cream?
  你的冰淇淋要淋糖浆吗？

- Could we take a look at the menu?
  我们能看一下菜单吗？

- This smells delicious.
  这闻起来好美味。

★ 换个单词说说看 | 用单词丰富句子，让句子更漂亮！

Additional Vocabulary & Phrases | 补充单词 & 短语

- **melt** v 融化
  The ice cube is melting quickly.
  冰块正在快速地融化。

- **coupon** n 折价券
  Do you have any coupons?
  你有折价券吗？

Daily Vocabulary 语言学校都会教的实用日常单词

1. fruity 水果味的

strawberry	[ˈstrɔːbəri] [n]	草莓
cherry	[ˈtʃeri] [n]	樱桃
melon	[ˈmelən] [n]	香瓜
mango	[ˈmæŋgəʊ] [n]	杧果
banana	[bəˈnɑːnə] [n]	香蕉
cranberry	[ˈkrænbəri] [n]	蔓越莓

2. flavor 口味、味道

coffee	[ˈkɒfi] [n]	咖啡
brownie	[ˈbraʊni] [n]	布朗尼
vanilla	[vəˈnɪlə] [n]	香草
mint chocolate	[ph]	薄荷巧克力
Swiss chocolate	[ph]	瑞士巧克力
green tea	[ph]	抹茶
rum and raisin	[ph]	朗姆葡萄
Macadamia nut	[ph]	夏威夷果

3. toppings 填料、调料

syrup	[ˈsɪrəp] [n]	糖浆	cinnamon	[ˈsɪnəmən] [n]	肉桂
fudge	[fʌdʒ] [n]	软糖	caramel	[ˈkærəmel] [n]	焦糖
toffee sauce	[ph]	太妃糖浆	whipped cream	[ph]	鲜奶油

4 ice cream sandwich 冰淇淋三明治

popsicle ['pɒpsɪkl] ······ 冰棒
ice cream cone ph ······ 冰淇淋蛋卷
soft-serve ice cream ph ······ 软冰淇淋

5 sundae 圣代冰淇淋

sorbet ['sɔːbeɪ] n ······ 雪糕、冰糕
（鲜果制成的冰沙甜品）
strawberry sundae ph ······ 草莓圣代
banana milkshake ph ······ 香蕉奶昔
frozen yogurt ph ······ 冻酸奶
scoop [skuːp] n ······ 冰淇淋勺
one scoop of ice cream ph ······ 一球冰淇淋

6 nuts 坚果

pecan [ˈpiːkən] n ······ 美洲山核桃
almond [ˈɑːmənd] n ······ 扁桃仁
cashew [ˈkæʃuː] n ······ 腰果
hazelnut [ˈheɪzlnʌt] n ······ 榛子
peanut [ˈpiːnʌt] n ······ 花生
pine nut ph ······ 松子、松仁

7 ice cream topping 冰淇淋的配料

cereal [ˈsɪərɪəl] n ······ 玉米片
waffle [ˈwɒfl] n ······ 华夫饼干
coconut [ˈkəʊkənʌt] n ······ 椰子
chocolate sprinkles ph ······ 巧克力豆
gummy bear ph ······ 小熊软糖

Daily Q&A

〔会话一〕
Q▶ **What flavors of ice cream do you have?**
你们有哪些口味的冰淇淋？
A▶ **We have at least 20 different flavors.**
我们至少有 20 种不同的口味。

〔会话二〕
Q▶ **Can I taste some blackberry sorbet?**
我可以试吃一些黑樱桃冰沙吗？
A▶ **No problem.**
没问题。

〔会话三〕
Q▶ **How much is a scoop of ice cream?**
一球冰淇淋多少钱？
A▶ **It's 90 dollars in a cone and 70 dollars in a cup.**
用蛋卷装的是 90 美元，用杯装的是 70 美元。

Proverbs & Idioms 地道谚语与惯用语 | 让句子锦上添花

break the ice 打破僵局，打破沉默
When I go to a party, it is hard for me to break the ice. I really don't know how to start the conversation with a stranger.
参加派对时，打破沉默对我而言很难。我真的不知该怎样先和陌生人交流。

ice something down 用冰降温
They are icing the coke down now.
他们正在冰镇可乐。

ice something over 覆盖子一层薄冰
In winter, the river will ice over.
冬天时，河上面会结一层薄冰。

on thin ice 处于危险状态中
It's a very dangerous case. Don't do it, or you will find yourself on thin ice.
这是很危险的事。不要做，不然你会很危险。

cut no ice with someone 对某人没影响
I don't care how people see me. They cut no ice with me.
我不管人们怎么看我，他们对我没影响。

cream of the crop 最棒的
Fiona is very smart and hardworking. She is cream of the crop at her school. She always gets the best scores on every test.
莫奥娜非常聪明和努力。她是全校最棒的。她每次考试总是得最高分。

ice queen 冷美人
Tiffany is known for her poker face. She is an ice queen.
蒂芙尼以她的扑克脸闻名。她是个冷美人。

tip of the iceberg 冰山一角
The problem that many people see is just the tip of the iceberg. There are many other hidden ones waiting to be found.
这个问题只是冰山一角。还有很多待发现的问题在那里。

ice palace 珠宝店
What can you afford to buy in that ice palace?
在珠宝店里有什么你能买得起的东西？

Unit 4 Go to a Bakery 面包店

Daily Conversation 日常对话 | 模拟真实的日常对话

02-04

A Their cookies are just freshly made from the oven. They are 6 for 20 dollars.
他们的饼干才刚出炉，六个售价 20 美元。

B Sounds like a good bargain. I want 12.
听起来很划算，我要 12 个。

A Look at the Swiss roll over there. They look delicious, too. I am thinking about buying one.
看看那边的瑞士卷，看起来很好吃，我在想要不要买一个。

B You can taste it before you buy it. They have food tasting at the counter.
你可以先试吃再买，柜台那边提供试吃。

A I am starting to love this bakery.
我渐渐喜欢这家面包店了。

B It's one of my favorite bakeries.
这是我最爱的面包店中的一家。

A You should have told me earlier. I am a cookie lover.
你应该早一点告诉我，我是一个饼干爱好者。

Additional Vocabulary & Phrases | 补充单词 & 短语

- **bargain** [n] 特价商品、便宜货
  These clothes are a real bargain.
  这些衣服真的很划算。

- **food tasting** [ph] 试吃
  This supermarket usually offers many food tastings on the weekend.
  这家超市在周末的时候都有很多试吃。

Daily Sentences 高频用句 | 一分钟学一句，不怕不够用

- Can I have the **pineapple roll**^{*1} next to the cake?
  我可以买蛋糕旁的凤梨卷吗？

- How many flavors do the cookies come in?
  饼干有多少种口味？

- What is the most popular bread at this bakery?
  这家面包店最受欢迎的面包是哪一种？

- Do you sell **gingerbread**^{*2}?
  你们卖姜饼吗？

- I can't resist the **temptation** of bread and cookies.
  我无法抗拒面包和饼干的诱惑。

- The cookies and bread are **freshly made** in the oven every two hours.
  饼干和面包每两小时新鲜出炉。

- The cookies of the bakery are very popular in town.
  这家面包店的饼干在镇上很受欢迎。

- The bakery invites a famous baker from the USA. He is **good at** making cookies.
  那家面包店邀请了一位来自美国的著名面包师傅，他很擅长做饼干。

- Let's go to get some cookies. I am hungry now.
  我们去买些饼干吧，我现在好饿！

★ 换个单词说说看 | 用单词丰富句子，让句子更漂亮！

Additional Vocabulary & Phrases | 补充单词 & 短语

- temptation [n] 诱惑
  He has been able to resist the temptation.
  他一直以来都能够拒绝诱惑。

- freshly made [ph] 新鲜现做
  They have various kinds of pie freshly made every day.
  他们每天都有很多种新鲜做的派。

- good at... [ph] 擅长于……
  She is good at playing the piano.
  她擅长弹琴。

Daily Vocabulary 语言学校都会教的实用日常单词

1 cake 蛋糕

blueberry cheesecake [ph]	蓝莓芝士蛋糕
marble cheesecake [ph]	大理石芝士蛋糕
carrot cake [ph]	胡萝卜蛋糕
blueberry mousse [ph]	蓝莓慕斯
chocolate cake [ph]	巧克力蛋糕
mango mousse [ph]	杧果慕斯

2 bread 面包

toast [təʊst] [n]	烤面包片
butterbread [ˈbʌtəbred] [n]	奶油面包
biscuit [ˈbɪskɪt] [n]	小面包
croissant [krwaˈan] [n]	羊角面包

3 pastry 酥皮点心

pie [paɪ] [n]	馅饼	egg roll [ph]	蛋卷
almond flakes [ph]	杏仁酥片	red bean green tea roll [ph]	红豆绿茶蛋糕卷
strawberry tart [ph]	草莓馅饼		
pineapple roll [ph]	凤梨卷		

4 utensil 器具

baking paper [ph]	烘焙纸
foil [fɔɪl] [n]	铝箔纸
mixing bowl [ph]	搅拌容器
scale [skeɪl] [n]	磅秤
measuring spoon [ph]	量匙
rolling pin [ph]	擀面棍

5 ingredient 原料

cream cheese [ph]	奶油芝士
whipping cream [ph]	鲜奶油
unsalted butter [ph]	淡黄油
baking soda [ph]	苏打粉
gelatin ['dʒelətɪn] [n]	明胶
baking powder [ph]	泡打粉
cocoa powder [ph]	可可粉

6 cookie 甜饼干

butter shortbread [ph]	黄油酥饼
gingerbread ['dʒɪndʒəbred] [n]	姜饼
coconut cookies [ph]	椰子饼干
oatmeal cookies [ph]	燕麦饼干
mixed sesame cookies [ph]	黑白芝麻饼干

7 **cupcake** 杯子蛋糕

scone [skɒn] [n]		司康饼
cheese stick [ph]		芝士条
waffle ['wɒfl]		华夫饼
upside down cake [ph]		反转蛋糕
doughnut ['dəʊnʌt] [n]		甜甜圈

8 **baker** 面包（糕点）师傅

bake [beɪk] [v]		烘、烤
heat up [ph]		加热
cook [kʊk] [v]		烹煮
mix [mɪks] [v]		混合
freeze [friːz] [v]		冷冻
melt [melt] [v]		熔化
pour [pɔː] [v]		倒入
coat [kəʊt] [v]		涂在上面
preheat [ˌpriːˈhiːt] [v]		预热

Daily Q&A

〔会话一〕

Q▸ How do you like the cake?
你觉得蛋糕怎么样？

A▸ It is very delicious.
很可口。

〔会话二〕

Q▸ How much are the cookies?
饼干多少钱？

A▸ They are 6 for 20 dollars.
6个20美元。

〔会话三〕

Q▸ Do you have any food tasting?
你们有试吃吗？

A▸ Sure. It's right over the corner.
当然有，在角落那里。

Proverbs & Idioms 地道谚语与惯用语 | 让句子锦上添花

someone's bread and butter 基本收入
Working as a bartender is his bread and butter.
做调酒师是他基本的收入来源。

bread always falls on the buttered side 祸不单行
Not only did my motorcycle break down on the road, but my cell phone was out of batteries. I think bread always falls on the buttered side.
我不只在半路上摩托车坏了，连手机也没电了。我想真的是祸不单行。

bread-and-butter letter （给主人或主办方的）道谢信
When I got back home from the international meeting, it took me two days to finish with some bread-and-butter letters.
我在国际会议结束后回家，花了将近两天的时间写完了我的道谢信。

cast one's bread upon the waters 无怨无悔地付出
Tina is casting her bread upon the waters, supporting her husband while he works on every of his projects.
每当蒂娜的老公在做计划时，蒂娜都无怨无悔地付出。

know which side one's bread is buttered on 知道经济来源于何处
I know which side our bread is buttered on.
我知道经济来源于何处。

have your cake and eat it too 又要马儿跑，又要马儿不吃草。
You can't have your cake and eat it too. If you want to have a better service, you need to pay more money.
你又要马儿跑，又要马儿不吃草。如果你想要更好的服务，你就需要付更多的钱。

icing on the cake 令人更兴奋的事、锦上添花
Fiona is my best friend and her visiting is definitely icing on the cake.
菲奥娜是我最好的朋友，她的来访当然是令人非常兴奋的事。

sell like hotcakes （产品）热卖、畅销
i-Phone 6 is so popular. It sold like hotcakes.
i-Phone 6 很受欢迎。它很热卖。

Unit 5 — Go to a Candy Shop 糖果店

Daily Conversation | 日常对话 | 模拟真实的日常对话

02-07

A A new candy shop just opened around the corner last week. They have a variety of candies and it is always full of people.
上星期，附近有一家糖果店刚刚开业，他们有各式各样的糖果，而且总是挤满了人。

B That sounds really attractive. Let's go to that candy shop now.
听起来很吸引人，我们现在去糖果店吧。

(At the candy shop)
（在糖果店里）

A Look at the candy bar over there. It is so colorful and tasty.
看那里的糖果柜，它们是如此丰富多彩和美味。

B They have lollypops, chocolate drops, fruit candy, mints, peanut brittle and toffee. They are in different colors and flavors.
他们有棒棒糖、巧克力豆、水果糖、薄荷糖、花生糖和太妃糖。它们有不同的颜色和口味。

A I want to get a big bag and buy a little of everything.
我想要拿一个大袋子，然后各种口味买一些。

B Me too!
我也要！

Additional Vocabulary & Phrases | 补充单词 & 短语

- **full of** [ph] 充满
  The room is full of kids.
  这房间都是小孩。

- **attractive** [a] 吸引人的、有吸引力的
  That beautiful woman is very attractive.
  那个漂亮的女人非常有吸引力。

- **colorful** [a] 鲜艳的、多姿多彩的
  This story book is very colorful.
  这本故事书多姿多彩。

- **tasty** [a] 可口的、美味的
  This cheesecake is very tasty.
  这块芝士蛋糕真的非常美味。

Daily Sentences 高频用句 | 一分钟学一句，不怕不够用
02-08

- I really can't live without **candy***¹.
  我真的不能没有糖果。

- I have a **cavity**. It's killing me. I think I must have eaten too much candy.
  我有蛀牙，痛死了。我觉得我一定是吃了太多的糖。

- You can still eat candy. What you need to do is watch the **calories**. Don't eat too much.
  你还是可以吃糖果的。你要做的只是要小心热量。不要吃太多。

- Christmas is coming. Let's go to buy some candy canes to **decorate** our Christmas tree.
  圣诞节快到了。我们买些拐杖糖果来装饰我们的圣诞树。

- I know a famous candy shop on the first floor in the department store.
  我知道有一家有名的糖果店在百货公司的一楼。

- You put an apple on a stick and cover it with a lot of toffee. It's tasty.
  你把苹果放在一根棍子上，然后加上太妃糖。很好吃。

- You can put some marshmallows in hot chocolate. It's tasty.
  你可以放一些棉花糖到热巧克力里，很好吃。

- Eat some candy can **boost** your energy.
  吃糖果可以让你充满活力。

- Some candy is made of fresh fruit juice and is very natural.
  有些糖果是用新鲜果汁做成的，非常天然。

★ 换个单词说说看 | 用单词丰富句子，让句子更漂亮！

candy*¹ 可以替换：

| chocolate 巧克力 | peanut butter cup 巧克力花生杯 | gummy candy 软糖 |

I really can't live without _____.
我真的不能没有_____。

Additional Vocabulary & Phrases | 补充单词 & 短语

- **cavity** [n] 蛀洞、蛀牙
  Brushing your teeth every day can prevent a cavity.
  每天刷牙能预防蛀牙。

- **calorie** [n] 卡路里
  Cathy is instructed to start a low calorie and low fat diet.
  凯茜被指示要开始执行低热量低脂的饮食习惯。

- **decorate** [v] 装饰
  My mom decorated the living room with flowers.
  妈妈用鲜花装饰客厅。

- **boost** [v] 推动、促进
  An energy drink can boost your energy through the day.
  能量饮料可以促使你一整天有动力。

Daily Vocabulary 语言学校都会教的实用日常单词

1 snack 零食

candied fruit [ph]		蜜饯
cookie ['kʊki] [n]		（甜的）饼干
cracker ['krækə] [n]		（咸的）饼干
jelly ['dʒeli] [n]		果冻
pretzel ['pretsl] [n]		椒盐脆饼

2 chocolate 巧克力

brownie ['braʊni] [n]		布朗尼
white chocolate [ph]		白巧克力
milk chocolate [ph]		牛奶巧克力
dark chocolate [ph]		巧克力
fudge [fʌdʒ] [n]		乳脂软糖

3 candy 糖果

candy bar [ph]	单独包装的块状糖		bubble gum [ph]	泡泡糖
mint [mɪnt] [n]	薄荷糖		cotton candy [ph]	棉絮状的棉花糖
chewing gum [ph]	口香糖			

④ marshmallow 棉花糖

- **caramel** ['kærəmel] [n] 焦糖
- **toffee** ['tɒfi] [n] 太妃糖；乳脂糖
- **peanut brittle** [ph] 花生糖
- **nougat** ['nu:ga:] [n] 奶油杏仁糖；牛轧糖

⑤ nut 坚果

- **pumpkin seeds** [ph] 南瓜子
- **sunflower seeds** [ph] 葵花子
- **pistachio nuts** [ph] 开心果
- **popcorn** ['pɒpkɔːn] [n] 爆米花

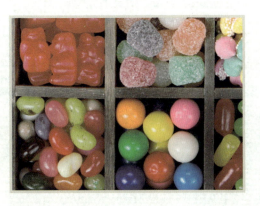

⑥ jelly beans 胶质软糖

- **gummy bear** [ph] 小熊软糖
- **candy cane** [ph] 拐杖糖
- **icing cookies** [ph] 糖霜饼干
- **lollipop** ['lɒlipɒp] [n] 棒棒糖
- **cranberry truffles** [ph] 蔓越莓松露

7 flavors 味道

taste [teɪst] v ……… 尝、辨（味）
sweet [swiːt] a ……… 甜的
sour [saʊə] a ……… 酸的
bitter ['bɪtə] a ……… 有苦味的
spicy ['spaɪsi] a ……… 多香料的、辛辣的
hot [hɒt] a ……… 辣的
salty ['sɔːlti] a ……… 咸的

8 unit 单位

bar [bɑː] n ……… 条、棒
bowl [bəʊl] n ……… 碗
piece [piːs] n ……… 片、块、张
slice [slaɪs] n ……… 片、份
box [bɒks] n ……… 盒
bag [bæg] n ……… 袋
gram [græm] n ……… 克
pound [paʊnd] n ……… 磅
kilogram ['kɪləgræm] n ……… 公斤
dozen ['dʌzn] n ……… 打
package ['pækɪdʒ] n ……… 包
liter ['liːtə] n ……… 升

Daily Q&A

〔会话一〕
Q▶ What flavor does the candy come in?
这些糖果有哪些口味？
A▶ It comes in strawberry and honey melon.
有草莓和哈密瓜口味。

〔会话二〕
Q▶ Have you tried toffee apple before?
你有没有吃过太妃糖苹果？
A▶ Nope. What is that?
没有，那是什么？

〔会话三〕
Q▶ What is your favorite candy?
你最喜欢的糖果是什么？
A▶ Gummy bears is my favorite.
我最喜欢小熊软糖。

Proverbs & Idioms 地道谚语与惯用语 | 让句子锦上添花

be like taking candy from a baby 像从婴儿身边拿走糖一般容易、易如反掌
Making a cup of good coffee is really easy. It is like taking candy from a baby to him.
泡一杯咖啡真的很简单,就好像从婴儿身边拿走糖一样容易。

be like a kid in a candy store 像小孩到糖果店一样快乐、兴奋无比
He is like a kid in a candy store. He cannot help trying everything he sees in this room.
他真的像小孩子到糖果店一样兴奋。他忍不住试了在房间里看到的每一样东西。

be eye candy 漂亮吸引目光的人或事物
Some people think Fiona is just eye candy. She cannot really be a good actress.
有些人觉得菲奥娜只是个漂亮的花瓶,她没办法真的成为一个好的女演员。

chocolate box 非常漂亮的事物
We drove through a series of chocolate box wooden houses on our way to the beach.
我们开车去海滩的路上,经过一整排漂亮的木造房屋。

toffee-nosed 高傲的
She is so toffee-nosed. She always thinks she is much better than other people.
她很高傲,总觉得她比别人都好。

sweet as honey 甜心、迷人的
Tina is sweet as honey. No wonder everyone loves her.
蒂娜很甜又迷人。难怪每个人都爱她。

sugar and spice 友善温柔
Sara can be all sugar and spice when she wants to be. But, she can also be pretty evil.
当莎拉想变得友善温柔时,她就可以完全地友善温柔。但是,她也可以变得相当邪恶。

Unit 6 Go to Burger Queen 快餐店

Daily Conversation 日常对话 ｜ 模拟真实的日常对话

A Let's go to Burger Queen for lunch. They have good cheese burgers.
我们去汉堡皇后吃午餐，他们有好吃的吉士汉堡。

B OK. I am hungry, too. I like their milkshake. They're very **creamy** and tasty.
好啊，我也饿了。我喜欢他们的奶昔，非常的香醇、浓郁。

(At Burger Queen) （在汉堡皇后）

A Look at the long line. There are always a lot of people waiting in line just for the cheese burgers. They must be very delicious.
看那长队，总是有很多人在那里排队买吉士汉堡，一定很好吃。

B Yup. But, this also means we have to wait to order our food.
是，但是这也意味着我们必须等候才能点餐。

A Come on. It is **worth** waiting. Their cheese burgers are really popular. Once you have it, you will love it.
拜托，这是值得等的。他们的吉士汉堡真的很受欢迎，一旦你吃过，你就会爱上。

B Well, sounds very **attractive**. I tried their **vanilla** milkshake last time, and it was really delicious.
嗯，听起来很吸引人。我上次喝过他们的香草奶昔，真的很好喝。

Additional Vocabulary & Phrases ｜ 补充单词 & 短语

- **creamy** [a] 奶香浓郁的、多乳脂的
  This pumpkin soup is very creamy.
  这个南瓜浓汤非常浓郁。

- **attractive** [a] 有吸引力的、引人注目的
  That beautiful woman is very attractive.
  那位美丽的女人很有吸引力。

- **worth** [a] 值得、有价值的
  That terrible movie is not worth watching.
  那部糟糕的电影不值得一看。

- **vanilla** [n] 香草
  Mandy loves vanilla ice cream.
  曼蒂非常喜欢香草冰淇淋。

Daily Sentences 高频用句 | 一分钟学一句，不怕不够用

- How many set meals do you have? What are they?
  你们有几种套餐？它们是什么？

- What drinks can I choose from for my set meal?
  我的套餐可以点什么饮料？

- We have 5 set meals. They are Big Cheeseburger, Giant Fish Burger, Big Chicken Burger, Chicken Nuggets, and Fried Chicken.
  我们有五种套餐，它们是大芝士汉堡套餐、巨无霸鱼堡套餐、大鸡堡套餐、鸡块套餐和炸鸡套餐。

- You can choose the dinks under 30 dollars.
  你可以点一杯低于 30 美元的饮料。

- Can I upgrade my drinks and my fries?
  我可以升级我的饮料和薯条吗？

- What's on the cheese burger*1?
  芝士汉堡里有什么？

- You can only upgrade one thing for every set meal.
  每一种套餐只能升级一种东西。

- I would like to have a large Coke*2.
  我想要一杯大杯可乐。

- Can I have the fried chicken with a chicken thigh only?
  我可以只要鸡大腿的炸鸡吗？

★ 换个单词说说看 | 用单词丰富句子，让句子更漂亮！

Additional Vocabulary & Phrases | 补充单词 & 短语

- set meal ph 套餐
  I would like to have the rice burger set meal.
  我想要米汉堡套餐。

- upgrade v 升级
  I got a flight upgrade last time when I went to Rome.
  上次我去罗马的时候我升舱了。

- thigh n 大腿
  I exercise every day in order to make my thigh slimmer.
  我为了瘦大腿所以每天运动。

Daily Vocabulary 语言学校都会教的实用日常单词

1 fast food 快餐

fast [fɑːst] a	快速的
convenience [kən'viːniəns] n	便利
chain-store restaurant ph	连锁餐厅
combo ['kɒmbəʊ] n	套餐
meal [miːl] n	一餐、膳食

2 hamburger 汉堡

cheeseburger ['tʃiːzbɜːgə] n	芝士堡
rice burger ph	米香堡
chicken sandwich ph	鸡肉三明治
fish burger ph	香鱼堡
veggie burger ph	蔬菜堡

3 fried chicken 炸鸡

chicken nugget ph	鸡块	hash brown ph	马铃薯饼
french fries ph	薯条	cheese sticks ph	芝士条
onion rings ph	洋葱圈		

4 snack and side 副餐点心

ice cream ph	······	冰淇淋
apple pie ph	······	苹果派
salad ['sæləd] n	······	沙拉
corn soup ph	······	玉米浓汤
yogurt ['jɒgət] n	······	酸奶

5 bacon 培根

ham [hæm] n	······	火腿
sausage ['sɒsɪdʒ] n	······	腊肠
pepperoni [,pepə'rəʊni] n	······	意大利辣腊肠
salami [sə'lɑːmi] n	······	意大利蒜味腊肠
lunch meat ph	······	冷肉（午餐肉）

6 drinks 饮料

Coke [kəʊk] n	······	可乐
iced tea ph	······	冰红茶
coffee ['kɒfi] n	······	咖啡
milkshake ['mɪlkʃeɪk] ph	······	奶昔
cocoa ['kəʊkəʊ] n	······	可可
juice [dʒuːs] n	······	果汁
milk [mɪlk] n	······	牛奶

7 ask 询问

straw [strɔː] [n] 吸管
napkin ['næpkɪn] [n] 纸巾
free-refill [ph] 免费续杯
hot [hɒt] [a] 热的
cold [kəʊld] [a] 冰的

8 sauce 调味酱

ketchup ['ketʃəp] [n]	番茄酱	pepper ['pepə] [n]		胡椒
mustard ['mʌstəd] [n]	芥末	salt [sɔːlt] [n]		盐
barbecue ['bɑːbɪkjuː] [n]	烤肉酱	sugar ['ʃʊɡə] [n]		糖
mayonnaise [ˌmeɪə'neɪz] [n]	蛋黄酱	chili sauce [ph]		辣酱
sweet and sour sauce [ph]	糖醋酱	pickled relish [ph]		酸黄瓜

Daily Q&A

〔会话一〕

Q ▶ What would you like to order?
你想要点什么？

A ▶ I would like to have a cheese burger.
我想要一个芝士汉堡。

〔会话二〕

Q ▶ For here or to go?
你想在这里吃，还是带走？

A ▶ To go, please.
带走。

〔会话三〕

Q ▶ Can I have some straws and mayonnaise?
可以给我一些吸管和蛋黄酱吗？

A ▶ Sure. There you go.
没问题，在这里。

Proverbs & Idioms 地道谚语与惯用语 | 让句子锦上添花

make hamburger out of someone 揍某人
If you don't behave well I will make hamburger out of you!
如果你不好好守规矩，我会揍你！

toss a salad 拌沙拉
The host tossed the salad in front of all the guests and served every one of them a plate of fresh salad.
主人在所有客人面前拌沙拉，然后在每个人的盘子上放一份新鲜的沙拉。

in one's salad days 在某人年轻时
Irene always recalls the joy she experienced on her school vacation in her salad days.
艾琳总是回想她年轻时学校放假时所经历过的愉快时光。

have one's finger in too many pies 参与太多事
You make yourself too busy by having your finger in too many pies.
你参与人事太多了，所以太忙了。

pie in the sky 不切实际的想法计划
Be realistic! Don't just make your plans like pie in the sky.
实际一点！不要只是在空中画大饼，做些不实际的计划。

bring home the bacon 工作赚钱养家
Jason is a father. He works very hard to bring home the bacon.
杰森是个父亲。他非常努力工作赚钱养家。

no spring chicken 不再是年轻小伙子
He is 58 years old now. He is no spring chicken.
他现在58岁了。他不再是一个年轻小伙子。

butter (someone) up 阿谀奉承
Jerry often butters up his boss in order to get the latest news about the policy of his company.
杰瑞常常阿谀奉承他的老板来获取公司政策方面的最新消息。

Unit 7 Go to a Sea Food Restaurant 海鲜餐厅

Daily Conversation | 日常对话 | 模拟真实的日常对话

A Let's go to the seafood restaurant in our **neighborhood**.
我们去我们家附近的那家海鲜餐厅。

B Sound great. Let's go! 听起来不错，我们走吧！

(At the seafood restaurant) （在海鲜餐厅）

A Look at the **crystal** clear fridge. You can see a variety of seafood in it. They all look very fresh and delicious.
看那清澈透明的冰箱，你可以看到里面有各式各样的海鲜，它们都看起来很新鲜、很可口。

B True. I would like to have some salmon sashimi and a roast salmon head.
真的！我想要吃一些鲑鱼生鱼片和烤鲑鱼头。

A You sound like a seafood **expert**. I would like to have some stir-fried squids and **steamed** shrimp.
你听起来像是个海鲜专家。我想要一些炒鱿鱼和清蒸虾。

B You are not too bad as well. I also want to have a steamed lobster. It really tastes like its from the heaven.
你听起来也不错！我还想点一只清蒸龙虾，它们吃起来美味极了。

Additional Vocabulary & Phrases | 补充单词 & 短语

- **neighborhood** n 邻近地区、邻居
  She lives around our neighborhood.
  她住得离我们家很近。

- **crystal** a 水晶的
  Dad uses his crystal glass to drink wine.
  爸爸用他的水晶杯喝红酒。

- **expert** n 专家
  She's an expert in baking.
  她在烘焙方面是个专家。

- **steam** v 蒸
  I want to steam some bun for breakfast.
  我想蒸一些馒头当早餐。

Daily Sentences 高频用句 | 一分钟学一句，不怕不够用

- Do you think we should try some deep fried oysters?
  你觉得我们要试试炸牡蛎吗？

- Oysters are tasty and contain a lot of nutrition.
  牡蛎很好吃，而且含有很多营养。

- I am allergic to seafood, and I dislike the smell. Whenever I have seafood, I will have diarrhea.
  我对海鲜过敏，而且我也不喜欢那个味道。我每次吃海鲜就会拉肚子。

- I would like my salmon*1 in a soup.
  我想要用鲑鱼煮汤。

- Eating oysters is good for your skin. They are nicknamed sea milk.
  吃牡蛎对你的皮肤好。它们有一个绰号叫作"海中牛奶"。

- You can tell the seafood from the color. If the color looks transparent, it is fresh.
  你可以从颜色判断海鲜。如果颜色看起来是透明的，就是新鲜的。

- Have you eaten sea urchin*2 before?
  你吃过海胆吗？

- I would like to have some clam chowder. It goes well with crackers.
  我想要喝一些蛤蜊浓汤，它们配苏打饼干很好吃。

- I would like to stir-fry some shellfish like clams, scallop, and mussels.
  我想要吃一些带壳的海鲜，像蛤蜊、扇贝，还有贻贝。

★ 换个单词说说看 | 用单词丰富句子，让句子更漂亮！

Additional Vocabulary & Phrases | 补充单词 & 短语

- **nutrition** [n] 营养、滋养
  Fish contains a lot of nutrition.
  鱼有很多营养。

- **allergic** [a] 过敏的
  I am allergic to nuts.
  我对坚果类过敏。

- **diarrhea** [n] 腹泻
  He suffered from diarrhea due to the milk.
  他因为喝了牛奶而腹泻。

- **nickname** [n] 昵称、绰号
  What's her nickname?
  她的绰号是什么？

Daily Vocabulary 语言学校都会教的实用日常单词

1 marine organism 海洋生物

octopus [ˈɒktəpəs] n		章鱼
squid [skwɪd] n		乌贼
cuttlefish [ˈkʌtlfɪʃ] n		墨鱼
urchin [ˈɜːtʃɪn] n		海胆
jelly fish ph		水母

2 fish 鱼

anchovy [ˈæntʃəvi] n		凤尾鱼
salmon [ˈsæmən] n		鲑鱼
bass [beɪs] n		鲈鱼
cod [kɒd] n		鳕鱼
tuna [ˈtjuːnə] n		金枪鱼

3 shellfish 贝、有壳的水生动物

oyster [ˈɔɪstə] n	牡蛎		**lobster** [ˈlɒbstə] n	龙虾
crab [kræb] n	螃蟹		**clam** [klæm] n	蛤蜊
shrimp [ʃrɪmp] n	虾		**scallop** [ˈskɒləp] n	扇贝

4 appearance 外观、外显

lively ['laɪvli] a ········· 活泼的
dead [ded] a ········· 死的
transparent [træns'pærənt] a ········· 透明的
fresh [freʃ] a ········· 新鲜的

5 negative 负面的

influence ['ɪnfluəns] n ········· 作用、影响
poison ['pɔɪzn] a ········· 有毒的
diarrhea [ˌdaɪə'rɪə] n ········· 腹泻
smell [smel] n ········· 臭味
disgusting [dɪs'gʌstɪŋ] a ········· 令人厌恶的
vomit ['vɒmɪt] v ········· 呕吐
dehydration [ˌdiːhaɪ'dreɪʃn] n ········· 脱水
stale [steɪl] a ········· 不新鲜的
rotten ['rɒtn] a ········· 发臭的、腐败的
expire [ɪk'spaɪə] v ········· 过期

6 cooking 烹饪

deal with [ph]		处理
saute ['səʊteɪ] [v]		嫩煎、炒
roast [rəʊst] [v]		烤、炙、烘
stir-fry ['stɜː,fraɪ] [v]		炒
sashimi ['sæʃɪmi] [n]		生鱼片

7 fish tail 鱼尾

fish eye [ph]	鱼眼		fin [fɪn] [n]	鱼鳍
fish mouth [ph]	鱼嘴		vent [vent] [n]	排气孔
gill [gɪl] [n]	鳃			

Daily Q&A

〔会话一〕

Q▶ How would you like your crab to be cooked?
你希望你点的螃蟹怎么烹调？

A▶ I would like it to be steamed.
我想用蒸的。

〔会话二〕

Q▶ Do you like seafood?
你喜欢海鲜吗？

A▶ Not really.
还好。

〔会话三〕

Q▶ How does the fish taste?
这些鱼尝起来如何？

A▶ They taste fantastic!
尝起来非常美味！

Proverbs & Idioms 地道谚语与惯用语 | 让句子锦上添花

happy as a clam　快乐
Since he has been in a university, he is happy as a clam.
因为他已经上大学了，他很快乐。

clam up　闭嘴
He promised not to tell anyone the secret, so when people asked him about the thing, he just clammed up.
他保证不会给任何人说这个秘密，所以只要有人问到这件事，他就闭嘴。

shut up like a clam　突然闭口不提
I was chatting happily with Jeremy. However, he shut up like a clam when I asked him something about his trip to Japan.
我正快乐地和杰瑞米聊天。然而，我一问到他这次到日本的旅行时，他却突然闭口不提。

a fish out of water　不适应新地方、如鱼没有水
After having lived in Taipei for almost all his life, he is like a fish out of water when staying in New York.
他一生中的大部分时间住在台北，他真的不太适应纽约的新环境，就好像鱼出了水一般。

fish tale　谎言
Kelly is a master at the fish tale. She should be a politician.
凯莉很擅长说谎，她很适合当一个政客。

fish around　在某处到处寻找
The boy fished around his pocket for some coins.
那男孩在他的口袋里寻找硬币。

fish in troubled waters　浑水摸鱼
Pay more attention to the class. Don't try to fish in troubled waters.
上课专心一点，不要老是浑水摸鱼。

Unit 8 Go to an American Restaurant 美式餐厅

Daily Conversation | 日常对话 | 模拟真实的日常对话

A Welcome to American Classic Restaurant. Did you make a <mark>reservation</mark>?
欢迎来到经典美式餐厅。你们订位了吗？

B Nope. Can we have a table for two?
没有。我们可以要一个两人的座位吗？

A Let me check. Yes, there is a table for two by the window. Just <mark>follow</mark> me. I will <mark>lead</mark> you to the table.
让我看看。有，有一个靠窗的两人座位。跟着我，我带你们到座位。

B Thank you very much.
非常感谢你。

A Here is the <mark>menu</mark>. What would you like to order?
这是菜单。你们想要点什么？

B We would like to order two set meals.
我们想要两份套餐。

Additional Vocabulary & Phrases | 补充单词 & 短语

- **reservation** [n] 预订
  We've made a reservation for a table at that restaurant.
  我们已经在那家餐厅订了一桌位。

- **follow** [v] 跟随
  The dog followed the cat to the garden.
  那只狗跟着那只猫去了花园。

- **lead** [v] 引领、领（路）
  She led us the way to the library.
  她带着我们到图书馆。

- **menu** [n] 菜单
  Can you ask the waiter to bring us the menu?
  你能请服务生帮我们送一下菜单吗？

Daily Sentences 高频用句 | 一分钟学一句，不怕不够用

- Does the main course come with **soup or salad***¹?
  主餐有附汤或沙拉吗？

- How do you like your steak? Medium-rare, medium, medium-well or well-done?
  你的牛排要几分熟？三分、五分、七分或全熟？

- Can I have some **pepper and salt***²?
  可以给我一些胡椒和盐吗？

- What do you feel like eating for the **starter***³?
  你的前菜要吃什么？

- I would like to have two salads.
  我想要两份沙拉。

- I would like to have one roast chicken and one steak.
  我想要一份烤鸡腿和一份牛排。

- We would like to have **coffee***⁴ for drinks.
  我们的饮料要咖啡。

- I would like my steak medium-well.
  我想我的牛排要七分熟。

- Do you want anything to drink?
  你们想要点什么饮料吗？

★ 换个单词说说看 | 用单词丰富句子，让句子更漂亮！

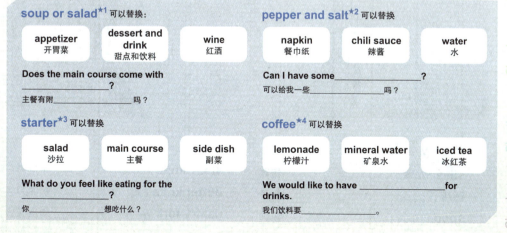

Daily Vocabulary 语言学校都会教的实用日常单词

1 atmosphere 气氛

cheerful	[ˈtʃɪəfl] a	快乐的
noisy	[ˈnɔɪzi] a	吵闹的
quiet	[ˈkwaɪət] a	安静的
graceful	[ˈgreɪsfl] a	典雅的
relax	[rɪˈlæks] a	轻松的
comfortable	[ˈkʌmftəbl] a	舒适的

2 table manners 餐桌礼仪

politeness	[pəˈlaɪtnəs] n	有礼貌
slurp	[slɜːp] v	出声地吃或喝
pass	[pɑːs] v	传递
order	[ˈɔːdə] v	点（餐）
elegant	[ˈelɪgənt] a	优雅的

3 cutlery 餐具

silverware	[ˈsɪlvəweə] n	银器	steak knife	ph	牛排刀
fork	[fɔːk] n	叉子	butter knife	ph	奶油刀
spoon	[spuːn] n	汤匙	pastry fork	ph	甜点叉

④ appetizer 开胃菜

aperitif [əˌperəˈtiːf] [n]	开胃酒	**finger food** [ph]	手抓小食品
chicken wing [ph]	鸡翅	**refined** [rɪˈfaɪnd] [a]	精致的
nachos [ˈnætʃəʊz] [n]	（墨西哥人食用的）烤干酪辣味玉米片		

⑤ main dish 主菜

- **steak** [steɪk] [n] ——— 牛排
- **pork** [pɔːk] [n] ——— 猪肉
- **chicken** [ˈtʃɪkɪn] [n] ——— 鸡肉
- **beef** [biːf] [n] ——— 牛肉
- **lamb chop** [ph] ——— 羊小排
- **barbecue** [ˈbɑːbɪkjuː] [n] ——— 烤肉

⑥ pasta 意大利面

- **lasagna** [ləˈzænjə] [n] ——— 千层面
- **spaghetti** [spəˈgeti] [n] ——— 意大利面条
- **rigatoni** [ˌrɪgəˈtəʊni] [n] ——— 通心粉
- **capellini** [n] ——— 天使细面
- **ravioli** [ˌræviˈəʊli] [n] ——— 意大利水饺

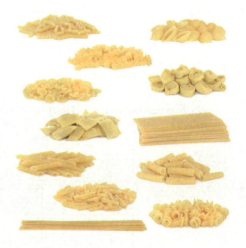

7 fruit 水果

dragon fruit [ph]	火龙果
honeydew [ˌhʌnidjuː] [n]	白兰瓜
bell-apple [ph]	甜椒
star fruit [ph]	杨桃
kiwi [ˈkiːwiː] [n]	奇异果

8 dessert 甜点

eclair [ɪˈkleə] [n]	长形泡芙	**panna cotta** [ph]	奶酪
souffle [n]	苏芙蕾	**chocolate fondant** [ph]	熔岩巧克力

Daily Q&A

〔会话一〕
Q▶ What do you feel like eating?
你想吃什么？
A▶ I feel like eating steak.
我想吃牛排。

〔会话二〕
Q▶ What is your favorite type of pasta?
你最喜欢哪种意大利面？
A▶ I like ravioli the best!
我最喜欢意大利水饺！

〔会话三〕
Q▶ What do you want for dessert?
你想要吃什么甜点？
A▶ I would like to have the panna cotta.
我想要奶酪。

Proverbs & Idioms 地道谚语与惯用语 | 让句子锦上添花

beef something up 加强
Let's beef up the music project with more money.
让我们给那个音乐计划增加更多的预算。

beef about 抱怨
Stop beefing about Helen. She didn't do that on purpose.
不要再抱怨海伦了,她不是故意那样做的。

have a beef with someone/something 认为某事或某人需要改变
I have a beef with those bad programs on TV.
我认为那些电视上不好的节目需要改善。

pork out 暴饮暴食
I am overweight now. I wish I had not porked out all the time for the past three weeks.
我现在超重了,我真希望我过去三周没有暴饮暴食。

like a lamb to the slaughter 如待宰的羔羊
The young solider went to the army like a lamb to the slaughter. Little did he know there was something dangerous waiting for him.
对那个年轻的军人来说,服兵役会让他如待宰的羔羊,他不知道一些危险的事情正在等着他。

Where's the beef? 实际的方法在哪里
That's really clever and appealing, but where's the beef? There's no substance in this proposal.
那真的很聪明又吸引人,但是实际的方法在哪里?这个策划书中没有一个实际的执行方法。

make lemonade out of lemons 苦中作乐
Since I've lost my job, I plan on making lemonade out of lemons. I want to start my own business!
既然我丢了工作,我就打算苦中作乐。我想要开始我的事业!

Unit 9 Go to a Chinese Restaurant 中国餐厅

Daily Conversation 日常对话 | 模拟真实的日常对话

A I know a good Chinese restaurant around here. Let's go there.
我知道这附近有一家很棒的中国餐厅，我们去那边吃点东西吧。

B That is a really good idea.
那真是一个好主意

A Let's order some food for lunch.
我们点一些食物当午餐吧。

B Would you like rice with minced meat?
你想要吃卤肉饭吗？

A I am more interested in eating oyster noodle thread.
我对牡蛎面比较有兴趣。

B Then, I will order a rice with minced meat. For the drink, I want the rice and peanut milk.
那么，我会点卤肉饭，至于喝的，我要点米浆。

A Good. I want the soy bean milk.
好。我想要豆浆。

Additional Vocabulary & Phrases | 补充单词 & 短语

- **mince** v 切碎、剁碎
  We have some minced beef in the freezer.
  我们有一些碎牛肉在冷冻库里。

- **interested in** ph 对……有兴趣
  I am really interested in this movie.
  我对这部电影非常有兴趣。

- **thread** n 线、线状物
  There's a piece of thread on your hair.
  你的头发上有一小条线。

- **soy bean** ph 黄豆
  Tofu is made from soy bean.
  豆腐是黄豆做的。

Daily Sentences | 高频用句 | 一分钟学一句，不怕不够用 🎧 02-20

- Can you eat with **chopsticks**?
  可以用筷子吃饭吗？

- Can you recommend some delicious dishes?
  你可以推荐我一些好吃的菜品吗？

- Do you have **Peking duck***1 on the menu?
  你们的菜单上有北京烤鸭吗？

- What dish is popular in your restaurant?
  你们餐厅里哪些菜受欢迎？

- Can I share the table with other people?
  我可以和别人坐一桌吗？

- Can I have some chili sauce and vinegar?
  可以给我一些辣椒和醋吗？

- Let's sit around the table and ask the waiter to come and **serve** us.
  我们围着桌子坐，请服务生来为我们服务。

- My tummy is **grumbling**. I would like to have a **scallion pancake***2.
  我的肚子饿得呱呱叫。我想吃些葱油饼。

- There are so many people in the restaurant. I think we have to share the table with the couple over there. **Otherwise**, it may take ages for us to get a table.
  餐厅里有好多人，我想我们要跟那边的夫妻共坐一张桌子了，要不然我们要花上一辈子等座位。

★ 换个单词说说看 | 用单词丰富句子，让句子更漂亮！

Peking duck*1 可以替换：

| General Zhou chicken 左宗棠鸡 | cashew chicken 腰果鸡丁 | chow mein 炒面 |

Do you have _____ on the menu?
你们的菜单上有_____吗？

scallion pancake*2 可以替换：

| plate of stinky tofu 一盘臭豆腐 | glass of bubble tea 一杯珍珠奶茶 | bowl of beef noodle 一碗牛肉面 |

I would like to have a _____.
我想吃_____。

Additional Vocabulary & Phrases | 补充单词 & 短语

- **chopstick** [n] 筷子
  Many westerners don't know how to use chopsticks.
  很多西方人不知道怎么用筷子。

- **serve** [v] 为……服务、供应
  The waiter served me a glass of water.
  那个服务生为我上一杯水。

- **grumble** [v] 发出轰隆声、发出咕哝声
  She's grumbling about the bad weather.
  她正因为糟糕的天气发出咕哝声。

- **otherwise** [ad] 否则
  You need to go to bed early; otherwise you will get tired tomorrow.
  你要早点上床睡觉，否则你明天会很累。

Daily Vocabulary 语言学校都会教的实用日常单词

1 table 餐桌

round	[raʊnd] [a]	圆形的
square	[skweə] [n]	正方的
rectangle	['rektæŋgl] [n]	长方形
rotate	[rəʊ'teɪt] [v]	旋转
together	[tə'geðə] [a]	一起、共同
menu	['menjuː] [n]	饭菜、菜单

2 tea 茶

Woolong tea	[ph]	乌龙茶
osmanthus tea	[ph]	桂花茶
puer tea	[ph]	普洱茶
Biluochun	[n]	碧螺春
Long Jing Tea	[ph]	龙井茶
Tieguanyin	[n]	铁观音

3 staple 主食

rice	[raɪs] [n]	米饭
noodle	['nuːdl] [n]	面
sliced noodles	[ph]	刀削面
fried rice	[ph]	炒饭
fried noodles	[ph]	炒面
ramen	[ph]	拉面
beef noodles	[ph]	牛肉面

④ Dimsum 港式点心

dumpling ['dʌmplɪŋ] [n]	水饺
spring roll [ph]	春卷
sweet and sour pork [ph]	糖醋排骨
hot and sour soup [ph]	酸辣汤

⑤ soup 汤羹

sesame paste [ph]	芝麻糊
red bean soup [ph]	红豆汤
green bean soup [ph]	绿豆汤
tapioca [ˌtæpiˈəʊkə] [n]	西米露

⑥ hot pot 火锅

broths [brɒθ] [n]	汤头
rice noodle [ph]	米粉
green bean noodle [ph]	冬粉
tofu ['təʊfuː] [n]	豆腐
hot and spicy hot pot [ph]	麻辣火锅

7 oyster omelet 蚵仔煎

scallion pancake [ph]	葱油饼
rice with minced meat [ph]	卤肉饭
oyster noodle thread [ph]	蚵仔面
pig's blood rice pudding [ph]	猪血糕

8 breakfast 早餐

Chinese omelet [ph]	蛋饼	deep-fried Chinese donut [ph]	油条
fried leek dumpling [n]	韭菜盒子	sesame flat bread [ph]	烧饼
steamed bun [ph]	馒头	soybean milk [ph]	豆浆
steamed dumpling [ph]	蒸饺	rice and peanut milk [ph]	米浆
rice ball [ph]	饭团		
rice congee [ph]	粥		

Daily Q&A

〔会话一〕

Q▶ Can I have a pot of Woolong tea?
我可以点一壶乌龙茶吗?

A▶ Just a moment, please.
请等一下。

〔会话二〕

Q▶ Do you fancy some sesame paste?
你想吃芝麻糊吗?

A▶ Sure.
好啊。

〔会话三〕

Q▶ What would you like to have for breakfast?
你想要吃什么早餐?

A▶ I would like to have a scallion pancake with an egg and a soy bean milk.
我想要葱油饼加蛋,和一杯豆浆。

Proverbs & Idioms 地道谚语与惯用语 | 让句子锦上添花

strike it lucky 有突然来的好运
She struck it lucky with her first book which became an immediate best-seller.
她突如其来的好运，让她的第一本书马上就成为畅销书。

thank one's lucky stars 感谢某人的幸运星
I thanked my lucky stars. I studied the right things for the test.
我感谢我的幸运星，我刚好读到考试要考的东西。

lucky dog 幸运的人
You won the lottery?! You lucky dog!
你中乐透奖了吗？你这个幸运的人！

it is better to be born lucky than rich 出生富裕不如出生幸运
Maybe your family is not rich. But you are still lucky. You know it is better to be born lucky than rich.
你的家庭可能不富有，但你还是很幸运的。你要知道，出生富裕不如出生幸运。

lucky at cards, unlucky in love 牌运亨通，情场失利
Jack always won lots of money in the card games. However, it is always said that lucky at cards, unlucky in love. I think God is fair on everything.
杰克总是在玩牌时赢很多钱，然而俗话说："牌运亨通，情场失利。"我想上天总是公平的。

like the white on rice 就像白色在米上面没有什么差别
Those two colors are really close—like the white on rice.
那两个颜色真的很相近，没有什么差别。

noodle around 到处晃晃
I couldn't find the signs so I noodled around until I found the right address.
我无法找到指示标，所以只好到处晃晃，直到我找到正确的地址。

You cannot get blood from a turnip. 徒劳无功或无济于事的事
The government can't increase taxes any further—nobody has the money! You can't get blood from a turnip.
政府没办法再征收更多的税 —— 没有人有钱缴税！你不能做无济于事的事。

Unit 10 Go to a Coffee Shop 咖啡店

Daily Conversation | 日常对话 | 模拟真实的日常对话

A I'll go to find a place for us. Can you order an iced latte and a waffle with honey?
我去找我们的座位。你可以帮我点一杯冰拿铁和蜂蜜华夫饼干吗？

B Sure. I think I will have a cappuccino and some pancakes.
好的。我想要一杯卡布奇诺和一些美式松饼。

A It did not take a long time waiting for the food.
食物上来得很快。

B That is true. Their service is very fast. Do you want to read a magazine or newspaper?
的确，他们的上菜速度很快。你想看杂志或报纸吗？

A Yup. I had better catch up on the latest news, or I will become really outdated.
当然，我最好知道一些最新的消息，否则我会落伍的。

B Me too. It's been three days. I did not have enough time to read the news. I needed to finish my report this morning.
我也是。我已经有三天没有时间看新闻了，我今天早上需要完成我的报告。

A Let's enjoy our coffee and reading!
让我们享受我们的咖啡和阅读吧！

Additional Vocabulary & Phrases | 补充单词 & 短语

- **honey** [n] 蜂蜜
  I'd like to have some hot tea with honey.
  我想要喝些热茶加蜂蜜。

- **catch up** [ph] 跟上、赶上
  I am really behind on my class. I need to catch up.
  我在班上真的很落后了，我得赶紧跟上进度。

- **outdated** [a] 过时的
  That outfit is really outdated.
  那件衣服真的很过时。

- **report** [n] 报告
  I have a final report to finish.
  我有一份期末报告要完成。

Daily Sentences 高频用句 | 一分钟学一句，不怕不够用

- Is the coffee shop self-catering or does it have clerks to wait on the customers?
  这家咖啡店是自助式的，还是店员会为客人服务？

- Do you want some sugar*¹ in your coffee?
  你想要加一些糖到你的咖啡里吗？

- We have a beef bagel special and salmon bagel special. All the specials are served with an boiled egg and a regular coffee*².
  我们有牛肉贝果特餐、鲑鱼贝果特餐。所有的特餐都附送一颗水煮蛋和一杯中杯咖啡。

- I prefer strong coffee to weak coffee.
  我喜欢浓咖啡胜于淡咖啡。

- Cake usually tastes better with coffee.
  蛋糕配咖啡会更好吃。

- Would you like to sit inside or outside the coffee shop?
  你喜欢坐在咖啡店里面还是外面？

- I am a coffee lover. I cannot live without drinking coffee.
  我是一个咖啡爱好者，我不喝咖啡就活不下去。

- I can never resist the aroma of coffee.
  我永远无法抗拒咖啡的香味。

★ 换个单词说说看 | 用单词丰富句子，让句子更漂亮！

Additional Vocabulary & Phrases | 补充单词 & 短语

- **self-catering** a 自助式的
  This restaurant is self-catering.
  这家餐厅是自助式的。

- **boiled** a 煮沸的
  The water is boiled. Don't touch it!
  那水已经煮沸了。别碰它！

- **prefer** v 宁可、更喜欢……
  I prefer not to think about the past.
  我宁可不去想过去的事情。

- **resist** v 抗拒、拒绝
  I cannot resist the temptation of chocolate.
  我无法抗拒巧克力的诱惑。

Daily Vocabulary 语言学校都会教的实用日常单词
02-24

1 coffee 咖啡

coffee latte [ph]	拿铁
cappuccino [ˌkæpuˈtʃiːnəʊ] [n]	卡布奇诺
mocha [ˈmɒkə] [n]	摩卡
espresso [eˈspresəʊ] [n]	浓缩咖啡
iced coffee [ph]	冰咖啡

2 coffee mill 咖啡豆研磨机

espresso machine [ph]	意式咖啡机
brew [bru] [v]	煮（咖啡）
grind [graɪnd] [v]	磨（碎）、磨（成）
pour-over iced coffee brewer [ph]	冰滴咖啡机
coffee press [ph]	咖啡滤压壶

3 taste 尝

| caffeine [ˈkæfiːn] [n] | 咖啡因 | acidity [əˈsɪdəti] [a] | 酸度 |
| aroma [əˈrəʊmə] [n] | 香味 | body [ˈbɒdi] [a] | 浓度 |

4 coffee bean 咖啡豆

roast spectrum [ph] ···········烘焙色谱
blonde roast [ph] ············黄金烘焙
medium roast [ph] ···········中度烘焙
dark roast [ph] ··············深度烘焙

5 preference 偏爱

condense [kənˈdens] [v] ········浓缩
mixed [mɪkst] [a] ···············混合的
decaffeinated [ˌdiːˈkæfɪneɪtɪd] [a]
················无咖啡因的
low-fat milk [ph] ················低脂牛奶
milk foam [ph] ···················奶泡

6 flavors 味道

syrup [ˈsɪrəp] [n] ···············糖浆
caramel [ˈkærəmel] [n] ·········焦糖
cinnamon [ˈsɪnəmən] [n] ·······肉桂
vanilla [vəˈnɪlə] [n] ·············香草
cocoa [ˈkəʊkəʊ] [n] ············可可
peppermint [ˈpepəmɪnt] [n] ····胡椒薄荷

7 sandwich 三明治

bagel ['beɪgl] [n] ······ 硬面包圈
roast beef croissant [ph] 烤牛肉羊角面包
tuna sandwich [ph] ······ 鲔鱼三明治
egg salad sandwich [ph] 蛋沙拉三明治

8 tiramisu 提拉米苏

donut ['dəʊnʌt] [n] ······ 甜甜圈
muffin ['mʌfɪn] [n] ······ 玛芬
madeleine ['mædleɪn] [n] ······ 玛德琳蛋糕
cinnamon bun [ph] ······ 肉桂卷
waffle ['wɒfl] [n] ······ 华夫饼干

puff [pʌf] [n] ······ 泡芙
mousse [muːs] [n] ······ 慕斯
pudding ['pʊdɪŋ] [n] ······ 布丁
sundae ['sʌndeɪ] [n] ······ 圣代
pancake ['pænkeɪk] [n] ······ 煎饼

Daily Q&A

〔会话一〕
Q▶ What kind of coffee would you like to have?
你想喝哪一种咖啡？

A▶ I would like to have a double espresso.
我想要一杯双倍浓缩咖啡。

〔会话二〕
Q▶ Do you want to have some room for the milk?
你要留一些空间加牛奶吗？

A▶ Yes, please.
是的。

〔会话三〕
Q▶ Do you want some sugar in your coffee?
你想要加一些糖到咖啡里吗？

A▶ No, thanks. I like black coffee without sugar.
不，谢谢，我喜欢黑咖啡，不加糖。

Proverbs & Idioms 地道谚语与惯用语 | 让句子锦上添花

not someone's cup of tea　不是某人的菜，不是某人所喜爱的东西
Reading books is really not my cup of tea. I prefer doing sports.
阅读真不是我喜欢的事情，我喜欢运动。

be in one's cup　酒醉时
When Jerry is in his cup, he would sit there and do nothing but laugh.
杰瑞喝醉的时候，会坐在那里什么事都不做并傻笑。

wake up and smell the coffee　注意并着手进行
The parents had better wake up and smell the coffee. It is very obvious that their children have got some serious problems.
这对父母最好要做一些事情了。很明显，他们的孩子有一些严重的问题。

the flavor of the mouth　暂时或目前普遍流行
The first music album of the rap artist just released and it suddenly became the flavor of the mouth.
这位饶舌歌手的第一张音乐专辑刚发行，就马上变成目前最流行的音乐。

it's no use crying over spilled milk　木已成舟，于事无补
I know you do not like your new hairstyle, but you can't change it since it is no use crying over spilled milk.
我知道你不喜欢新发型，但是你没有办法改变了，因为木已成舟，于事无补。

milk a duck　给鸭子挤牛奶（做不可能的事）
It is just like milking a duck. I can't do it!
这好像给鸭子挤牛奶。我不会！

land of milk and honey　像圣经中的应许之地、富饶的地方、鱼米之乡
Many people came to the United States thinking it was the land of milk and honey.
很多人来到美国以为它是富饶的地方，十分美好。

milk someone for something　索求
The thief milked me for 3 000 dollars.
那个小偷向我索要 3 000 美元。

Go to a Convenience Store 便利商店

Daily Conversation 日常对话 | 模拟真实的日常对话

02-25

A Gee... I am so hungry. I want to get something to eat at the convenience store.
天哪！我好饿，我想到便利店找一些东西吃。

B I know they now have some special offers.
我知道他们现在有特价。

A Do you want to come with me?
你想跟我一起去吗？

B Why not? I need some stationery. I ran out of paper and ball point pens.
好呀！我想买一些文具用品。我的纸和圆珠笔都没有了。

A I want to buy a hot dog, a tea egg and some oden.
我想买一份热狗、一个茶叶蛋和一些关东煮。

B Do you want me to get a drink for you? The stationery section is right next to the fridge.
你要我帮你拿些喝的吗？文具区就在冰箱的隔壁。

A OK. I want a bottle of coke.
好呀！我要一瓶可乐。

Additional Vocabulary & Phrases | 补充单词 & 短语

- **convenience** n 方便、合宜
  Do you think Jane is making a convenience of Lily?
  你觉得珍在利用莉莉吗？

- **offer** v 给予、提供
  She offered me a cup of hot tea.
  她给我一杯热茶。

- **run out of** a 用完、耗尽
  We've ran out of toilet paper.
  我们的卫生纸用完了。

- **bottle** n 瓶子
  There's a bottle of water over there.
  那边有一瓶水。

Daily Sentences 高频用句 | 一分钟学一句，不怕不够用
02-26

- What kind of stationery is there at a convenience store?
  便利店卖哪些文具？

- What things are on special sale?
  哪种东西正在特价卖？

- The convenience store offers newspapers、glue、white-out、paper clips and even scissors.
  这家便利店有报纸、胶水、修正液、回形针，甚至剪刀。

- I bought something online. I would like to collect my goods here.
  我在网上买了一些东西。我想要在这里取这些商品。

- The ice cream is buy two get one free.
  冰淇淋买二送一。

- I usually buy my groceries at the convenience store.
  我通常在便利店买杂货。

- All drinks are buy one get the second 40% off.
  所有的饮料买一件后第二件六折。

- Can you get a pack of cigarettes ★1 for me?
  你可以拿一包香烟给我吗？

- I want to pay my telephone bill ★2.
  我想交电话费。

★ 换个单词说说看 | 用单词丰富句子，让句子更漂亮！

cigarettes ★1 可以替换：		
potato chips 薯片	chocolate 巧克力	chewing gum 口香糖

Can you get a pack of _____ for me?
你可以帮我拿一包 _____ 吗？

telephone bill ★2 可以替换：		
tuition 学费	insurance 保险费	credit card bill 信用卡费

I want to pay my _____.
我想要交 _____。

Additional Vocabulary & Phrases | 补充单词 & 短语

- white-out ph 修正液
  I've run out of white-out.
  我修正液用完了。

- goods n 商品、货物
  She sells handmade goods.
  她卖手工艺品。

- grocery n 食品杂货
  We need to buy some groceries this weekend.
  这个周末我们需要添购一些食品杂货。

- pack n 一包（盒、箱、袋）
  She gave me a pack of candy.
  她给我一包糖果。

067

Daily Vocabulary 语言学校都会教的实用日常单词

1 daily necessity 日常必需品

tissue paper [ph]	卫生纸
razor ['reɪzə] [n]	刮须刀
soap [səʊp] [n]	肥皂
hand moisturizer [ph]	护手霜
cleansing foam [ph]	洁面乳
shower gel [ph]	沐浴液
shampoo [ʃæm'puː] [n]	洗发水
hair conditioner [ph]	护发乳

2 canned food 罐头食品

potato chips [ph]	薯片
vinegar ['vɪnɪgə] [n]	醋
soy sauce [ph]	酱油
instant noodles [ph]	方便面
dried bean curd [ph]	豆干
expiration date [ph]	保质期

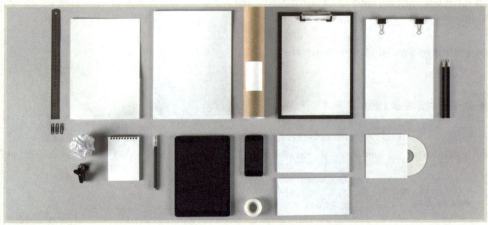

3 stationery 文具

knife [naɪf] [n]	刀	ink pens [ph]	签字笔
scissors ['sɪzəz] [n]	剪刀	glue [gluː] [n]	胶水
envelope ['envələʊp] [n]	信封		

4 delicatessen 熟食

oden [n]	关东煮
hot dog [ph]	热狗
tea egg [ph]	茶叶蛋
onigiri [n]	三角饭团
rice balls/fan tuan [ph]	中式饭团

5 counter 柜台、柜台式长桌

cashier [kæˈʃɪə] [n]	收银员
telephone bill [ph]	电话账单
gas bill [ph]	燃气费账单
utility bill [ph]	电费账单
water bill [ph]	水费账单

6 cigarettes 香烟

beer [bɪə] [n]	啤酒
wine [waɪn] [n]	红酒
sparkling wine [ph]	气泡酒
champagne [ʃæmˈpeɪn] [n]	香槟酒
rice wine [ph]	米酒

7 beverage 饮料

juice [dʒuːs] [n] 果汁
milk [mɪlk] [n] 鲜奶
green tea [ph] 绿茶
soda ['səudə] [n] 汽水
bottled water [ph] 瓶装水

8 magazine 杂志

newspaper ['njuːzpeɪpə] [n] 报纸
catalog ['kætəlɒg] [n] 目录
comic books [ph] 漫画
flyer ['flaɪə] [n] 广告传单

Daily Q&A

〔会话一〕
Q▶ **Can I pay my telephone bill here?**
我可以在这里付电话费吗?
A▶ **Sure.**
当然。

〔会话二〕
Q▶ **Do you sell cigarettes?**
你们卖香烟吗?
A▶ **Yes. We sell a variety of cigarettes.**
卖,我们卖各式各样的香烟。

〔会话三〕
Q▶ **Can I have some hot water?**
我可以要些热水吗?
A▶ **Here you are.**
给你。

Proverbs & Idioms 地道谚语与惯用语 ｜ 让句子锦上添花

foot the bill 〉 付账单

My boss took me out for lunch and the company footed the bill.
我的老板请我吃饭，公司会付账。

sell someone a bill of goods 〉 欺骗

What your mom tells you is always true. She will never sell you a bill of goods.
你妈妈告诉你的都是真的。她从来不会欺骗你。

a clean bill of health 〉 被证明公司营运良好或一个人身体健康

⇨ Jason got a clean bill of health from his doctor. He can live longer than 100.
杰森被医生证明身体健康，他可以活到 100 岁。

⇨ Burger Ding got a clean bill of health from the government. They have good and stable profits every year.
Ding 汉堡被政府证明营运良好，他们每年有既好又稳定的收入。

fit the bill 〉 到达所需标准或资格

If you want some exciting entertainments, the amusement park in Taichung will fit the bill.
如果你想要一些较刺激的娱乐，台中的一家游乐园会符合你的标准。

a whale of a bill 〉 很大一笔金额的账单

We went to a luxury French restaurant. We ran up a whale of bill at the restaurant.
我们去了一家豪华的法式餐厅，我们最后要付很大的一笔钱给餐厅。

pay the water bill 〉 上厕所

I will be right back with you as soon as I pay the water bill.
我上完厕所马上回来。

billie 〉 钞票

Do you have any billies on you?
你身上有一些钞票吗？

Everyday Sentences 语言学校独家传授的必备好句子

- I would like to copy something. Can you turn on the copy machine?
  我想要打印一些东西。可以帮我把打印机打开吗？

- I love the meal boxes at QK. They come in different types of food, such as oden, rice balls, sushi, sandwiches, congee and so on.
  我喜欢在 QK 买快餐。他们有不同种类的食物，例如关东煮、饭团、寿司、三明治和粥等。

- I really like BK convenience store.
  我真的很喜欢 BK 便利店。

- They offer a variety of sweets and delicatessen. I really want a hot dog and some oden.
  他们有各式各样的甜食和熟食，我真的很想吃一份热狗和一些关东煮。

- Welcome to BK convenience store.
  欢迎光临 BK 便利店。

- You can go to the aisle next to the snack section. There is some basic stationery. Go look whether you can find anything you want.
  你可以去零食区旁的走道，那里有一些基本的文具。看看有没有你想要的文具。

- I will get you a pack of cigarettes when I check out at the counter.
  我去柜台结账时会顺便帮你买包烟。

- What do you want for breakfast?
  你早餐想吃什么？

- I'd like a large latte.
  我要一大杯拿铁。

- Can I have some ketchup please?
  能给我些番茄酱吗？

MEMO

From AM-PM 从早到晚都用得到的必备好句子

- Be careful. The coffee is very hot.
  小心！这咖啡很烫。

- What kind of dumplings do they have?
  他们有哪种水饺？

- I'd rather not eat anything too spicy.
  我不想吃太辣的食物。

- I think I'll pass on the chicken feet.
  我想我不会吃凤爪。

- Is pig's blood good?
  猪血好吃吗？

- Do they serve pearl milk tea here?
  他们这有珍珠奶茶吗？

- They serve "family style" meal here.
  这里提供"家庭式"的食物。

- Do you know how to use chopsticks?
  你知道怎么用筷子吗？

- I don't know how to use chopsticks. Do they have forks?
  我不会用筷子，他们有叉子吗？

- I eat fast food all the time.
  我一直都是吃快餐。

- This hamburger is so juicy!
  这个汉堡肉汁多！

MEMO

- Does this fast food restaurant have a drive-through?
  这家快餐店有得来速吗？

- I'm on a diet. I can't eat fast food.
  我在减肥，不能吃快餐。

- These shoes are not very comfortable.
  这些鞋子穿起来不是很舒适。

- I need to buy a present for my mom.
  我要买礼物给我妈。

- I'm shopping for a present.
  我在采买礼物。

- Ohh…My stomach doesn't feel good after eating that.
  喔！吃完那个东西之后我的胃不太舒服。

- What did I just eat?
  我刚刚吃了什么？

- What is this drink made from?
  这饮料是用什么做的？

- Put your toys away.
  把你的玩具收好。

- Clean the floor, please.
  请把地板清理干净。

- Mom, let me help you.
  妈妈，让我来帮你。

MEMO

Chapter 3

Institutions, School & Work
办正经事的地方

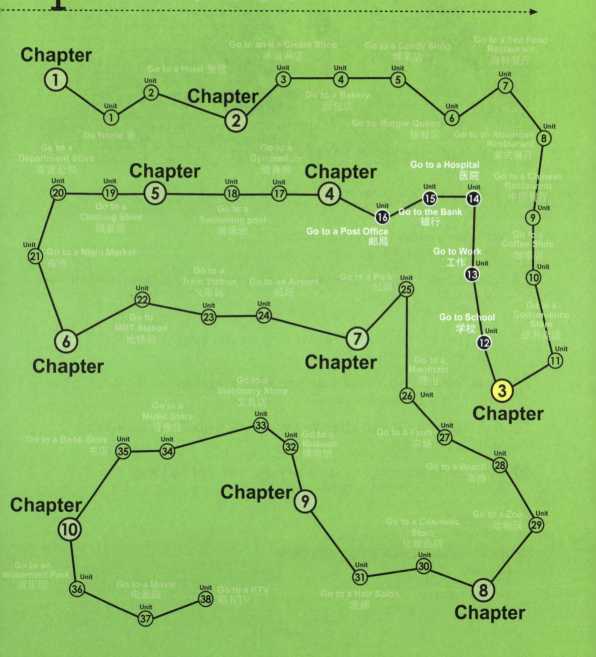

Unit 12 Go to School 学校

Daily Conversation 日常对话 | 模拟真实的日常对话

A Hi, Jenny. Are you going to school now?
嗨，珍妮。你现在要去上学吗？

B Yup. I have English at 9 in the morning.
是啊！我早上九点有英语课。

A I plan to look for some important books and study at the library. Do you want to join me?
我想在图书馆读书并找一些书。你要一起来吗？

B Sure. I need to return some books. They are due today.
好啊！我要还书。我的书今天到期了。

A Great. We can go to the swimming pool in the gymnasium after that.
太好了。我们之后可以去体育馆的游泳池。

B That sounds like a good idea. We can chill out a little in this hot weather.
很不错。我们可以在炎炎夏日中消暑一下。

A I am running late now. See you after class in front of the library then. Bye!
我快迟到了。那么下课后图书馆前见。再见！

B See you then.
到时候见。

Additional Vocabulary & Phrases | 补充单词 & 短语

- **due** [a] 到期的
  The report is due next Monday.
  这份报告下周一到期。

- **chill out** [ph] 冷静、让人放松
  This music can really chill me out.
  这个音乐真的能令我放松。

Daily Sentences 高频用句 | 一分钟学一句，不怕不够用

03-02

- What is your major?
  你主修什么？

- Who is the **president** *1 of this school?
  这所学校的校长是哪一位？

- Excuse me. Where and how can I **apply** for a library card? I would like to borrow some books.
  不好意思。我可以在哪里并且怎样申请一张图书馆卡？我想借一些书。

- What is the due date of these library books? I need to return them by the due date, or I will need to pay the **fine**.
  这些书几号到期？我要在到期前还书，不然我就得付罚金。

- At school, we need to follow the school **regulations**. We shall not **violate** those rules. Otherwise, we will be detained.
  在学校我们要遵守校规。我们不能违规，不然会被留校察看。

- I'm majoring in **Chemistry** *2.
  我主修化学。

- When do you finish your class?
  你什么时候上完课？

- Please hand in your homework on time every day.
  请每天准时交作业。

★ 换个单词说说看 | 用单词丰富句子，让句子更漂亮！

Additional Vocabulary & Phrases | 补充单词 & 短语

- **apply** v 申请
  I want to apply for the graduate program at Ohio State University.
  我想申请俄亥俄州立大学的硕士课程。

- **fine** n 罚金、罚款
  I need to pay for a $500 dollar fine.
  我需要交一笔 500 美元的罚金。

- **regulation** n 规章、规则
  We need to follow the regulation.
  我们必须遵守规则。

- **violate** v 违反、违背、侵犯
  The company was fined because they violated its customer's privacy.
  那个公司因为侵犯顾客的隐私而被罚款。

Daily Vocabulary 语言学校都会教的实用日常单词

1 classroom 教室

blackboard	[ˈblækbɔːd] [n]	黑板
whiteboard	[ˈwaɪtbɔːd] [n]	白板
eraser	[ɪˈreɪzə] [n]	板擦
chalk	[tʃɔːk] [n]	粉笔
desks and chairs	[ph]	课桌椅
wastepaper basket	[ph]	废纸篓
bell	[bel] [n]	钟声

2 sports field 操场

track and field	[ph]	田径
badminton	[ˈbædmɪntən] [n]	羽毛球
football	[ˈfʊtbɔːl] [n]	足球
dodge ball	[ph]	躲避球
track	[træk] [n]	运动跑道

3 playground 游戏场

swing	[swɪŋ] [n]	秋千	jungle gym	[ph]	攀爬架
seesaw	[ˈsiː sɔː] [n]	跷跷板	sand play area	[ph]	沙坑
the bars	[ph]	单杠			

④ library 图书馆

bookshelf ['bʊkʃelf] [n]		书柜
library card [ph]		借书证
overdue [,əʊvə'djuː] [a]		逾期的
solemn silence [ph]		保持肃静
novel ['nɒvl] [n]		小说
journal ['dʒɜːnl] [n]		期刊
quarterly publication [ph]		季刊
weekly publication [ph]		周刊
monthly publication [ph]		月刊

⑤ curriculum 学校全部课程大纲

mathematics [ˌmæθəˈmætɪks] = math [mæθ] [n]		数学
history ['hɪstri] [n]		历史
English ['ɪŋglɪʃ] [n]		英文
Chinese [ˌtʃaɪˈniːz] [n]		中文
chemistry ['kemɪstri] [n]		化学
physics ['fɪzɪks] [n]		物理
science ['saɪəns] [n]		科学
literature ['lɪtrətʃə] [n]		文学
biology [baɪˈɒlədʒi] [n]		生物
art [aːt] [n]		美术
P.E. = Physical Education [ph]		体育
geography [dʒiˈɒgrəfi] [n]		地理

6 **gymnasium** 体育馆

swimming pool ph	游泳池	**baseball field** ph	棒球场
gymnastics [dʒɪmˈnæstɪks] n	体操	**football field** ph	足球场
basketball court ph	篮球场	**golf course** ph	高尔夫球场
tennis court ph	网球场		

7 **faculty** 教职员

staff [stɑːf] n	行政人员
professor [prəˈfesə] n	教授
associate professor ph	副教授
assistant professor ph	助理教授
instructor [ɪnˈstrʌktə] n	讲师
teaching assistant ph	教学助理
chair professor ph	讲座教授
chair [tʃeə] n	系主任

Daily Q&A

〔会话一〕
Q▸ Are you good at playing golf?
你擅长打高尔夫球吗?
A▸ Yes, I am good at playing it.
是的,我很会打。

〔会话二〕
Q▸ What time does your school start?
你们学校几点开始上课?
A▸ It starts at 7:00 am.
早上七点开始。

〔会话三〕
Q▸ Which subject do you like the most?
你最喜欢哪一科?
A▸ I like English the most.
我最喜欢英文。

Proverbs & Idioms 地道谚语与惯用语 | 让句子锦上添花

cut class/cut school 翘课
Jane was punished because she cut school in order to join the party.
简因为逃课去派对而被处罚了。

from the old school 老派的
Aunt Helen is from the old school. She loves to wear a colorful long skirt.
海伦阿姨很老派。她喜欢穿彩色的长裙。

school of hard knocks 从艰苦中学习经验
Jeff did not go to school, but he went to the school of hard knocks. He learned things by his experience.
杰夫没有上过学,但是他在他的困难中学习成长。他从经验中学习。

tell tales out of school 散布谣言和秘密
Don't trust what Jimmy says. He never stops telling tales out of school.
别相信吉米说的话。他从没停止散布不实的话和消息。

the old school tie 旧校友关系网、校友人际关系
The old school tie still has enormous power when you work in some big companies.
当你到大公司工作时,校友人际关系有着很重大的影响。

schoolboy humor 幼稚的笑话
Come on! The joke is not funny at all. That is really schoolboy humor.
拜托!这个笑话一点也不好笑。真的是个幼稚的笑话。

pass with flying colors 高分通过考试
Greg studied really hard and he passed the final exam with flying colors.
格雷格读书很用功。他高分通过了期末考试。

teacher's pet 善于取悦老师的人
Frank is definitely teacher's pet. He always knows what to say to make our teacher happy.
法兰克当然是老师的宠儿。他总是知道说什么来取悦老师。

Unit 13 Go to Work 工作

Daily Conversation | 日常对话 | 模拟真实的日常对话

03-04

A Good morning, Mr. Smith.
早安，史密斯先生。

B Good morning, Jamie. What time is it now?
早安，杰米。现在几点了？

A It is 9 o'clock now.
现在九点整。

B I see. What is today's **schedule**?
我知道了。今天的行程是什么呢？

A You have two meetings today. One is at 10 am, and the other is at 2 pm.
你今天有两个会议。一个在早上十点，另一个在下午两点。

B OK. Can you **prepare** things for the meeting in the **conference** room? Make enough copies of the **handouts**.
好。你可以帮我在会议室准备会议所需要的物品吗？准备足够的提纲讲义。

A No problem. 没问题。

Additional Vocabulary & Phrases | 补充单词 & 短语

- **schedule** [n] 行程表、课程表
  What is your class schedule next semester?
  你下学期的课表是什么？

- **prepare** [v] 准备
  Can you prepare some apple juice for your sister?
  你能帮你姐姐准备一些苹果汁吗？

- **conference** [n] 会议、讨论会
  The professor will give a speech at the annual conference.
  那位教授会在年度讨论会上演讲。

- **handout** [n] 讲课题纲、讲义
  Please make 30 copies of handout for the class.
  这堂课请准备 30 份的讲义。

Daily Sentences 高频用句 | 一分钟学一句，不怕不够用

- Can you fax this to Mr. Chen by 9 o'clock?
  你可以在 9 点前把这份文件传真给陈先生吗？

- Hello, can you make a phone call to Mr. Brown and set up the meeting time?
  你好，你可以打电话给布朗先生并确定会议时间吗？

- We are going to have a meeting about the contract with BMY at 9 am.
  我们将在早上 9 点和 BMY 进行关于合同的会议。

- Excuse me, can you tell me where the **copy machine** [1] is?
  不好意思，你可以告诉我打印机在哪里吗？

- Those are used documents. Please destroy them by using the paper shredder because they contain some important information.
  那些都是用过的资料。请用碎纸机销毁，因为那些资料含有重要信息。

- BMY is a very big company. There are 200,000 employees in this company.
  BMY 是一家非常大的公司。这家公司有 200 000 名员工。

- In the meeting, I want to briefly show my ideas by using the OHP.
  在这次会议中，我想要用投影机简单地展示我的想法。

- Can you put those **files** [2] in the cabinet over there?
  你可以将这些文件放置在那边的柜子中吗？

- Please ask the receptionist to wait for an important customer at the reception counter.
  请叫接待员在接待处等候重要的贵宾。

★ 换个单词说说看 | 用单词丰富句子，让句子更漂亮！

Daily Vocabulary 语言学校都会教的实用日常单词

① office 办公室

reception counter [ph]	服务台
receptionist [rɪˈsepʃənɪst] [n]	接待员
meeting room [ph]	会议室
meeting table [ph]	会议桌
office cubicle [ph]	办公室隔间

② boss 老板

secretary [ˈsekrətri] [n]	秘书
assistant [əˈsɪstənt] [n]	助手
employee [ɪmˈplɔɪi:] [n]	员工
staff [stɑːf] [n]	员工
customer [ˈkʌstəmə] [n]	顾客

③ facsimile(fax) machine 传真机

传真机内的功能键：

stop [stɒp] [v]	停止	hold [həʊld] [v]	暂停
exit [ˈeksɪt] [v]	退出	caller ID [ph]	来电显示
search [sɜːtʃ] [v]	寻找	quick-scan [ph]	快速扫描
speed dial [ph]	快速拨号	receive mode [ph]	接收模式

4 **photocopier** 打印机

resolution [ˌrezə'luːʃn] n	解析度
time recorder ph	打卡机
paper cutter ph	裁纸机
shredder ['ʃredə] n	碎纸机
telephone ['telɪfəʊn] n	电话机
laminating machine ph	层压机
laminator film ph	塑封膜
overhead projector (OHP) ph	投影机

5 **filing cabinet** 资料柜

stapler ['steɪplə] n	订书机
file folder ph	资料夹
paper clip ph	回形针
glue [gluː] n	胶水
correction pen/tape ph	修正液/带
rubber ['rʌbə] n	橡皮擦

6 **drinking fountain** 饮水机

soda fountain ph	汽水饮料机
water dispenser ph	饮水机
vending machine ph	自动售卖机
lunch break ph	午餐休息时间

7 salary 薪水

- **promotion** [prə'məʊʃn] [n] ……… 升职
- **absent** ['æbsənt] [a] ……… 缺席的
- **sick leave** [ph] ……… 病假
- **vacancy** ['veɪkənsi] [n] ……… 空缺
- **layoff** ['leɪɔːf] [n] ……… 临时解雇

8 computer 电脑

- **mouse** [maʊs] [n] ……… 鼠标
- **printer** ['prɪntə] [n] ……… 打印机
- **computer virus** [ph] ……… 电脑病毒
- **memory disc** [ph] ……… 存储盘
- **CD burner** [ph] ……… 刻录机
- **Internet** ['ɪntənet] [n] ……… 互联网
- **wireless** ['waɪələs] [n] ……… 无线网
- **modem = modulator - demodulator** [ph] ……… 调制解调器
- **software** ['sɒftweə] [n] ……… 电脑软件

Daily Q&A

〔会话一〕
Q▶ What time is the meeting?
会议是什么时候呢？
A▶ 10 o'clock.
10 点钟。

〔会话二〕
Q▶ What is this meeting about?
这个会议是关于什么的呢？
A▶ It's about our new CEO.
是关于我们新总裁的。

〔会话三〕
Q▶ Do you need the OHP for the meeting?
你开会时要用投影机吗？
A▶ Yes.
是的。

Proverbs & Idioms | 地道谚语与惯用语 | 让句子锦上添花

All work and no play makes Jack a dull boy. 　工作与休闲要并重

Don't always sit at the computer and think about work only. All work and no play makes Jack a dull boy. Have fun sometimes!

不要整天只想坐在电脑前工作。工作与休闲要并重。有时候要做一些有趣的事。

Many hands make light work. 　众人拾柴火焰高

Cleaning the room will not take long if we all help. You know, many hands make light work.

如果我们帮忙的话，打扫房间不会花很久的时间。你知道的，有很多人协助可以轻松完成一份工作。

work like a dog 　忙碌工作中

Jack needs money to buy a house. He works like a dog every day.

杰克需要钱买一间房子。他每天都忙得像狗一样。

A little hard work never hurt/killed anyone. 　达成目标之前都得努力

Don't be afraid of difficulties. A little hard work never hurt/killed anyone. Just do your best!

别害怕困难。达成目标之前都得努力。只要尽力就好！

donkey work/hard work 　困难的工作

Why do I have to do all the donkey work and you can just sit there and enjoy your TV?

为什么我必须做所有困难的事而你只坐在那看你的电视？

show someone who's the boss. 　让某人知道谁才是做决定的人

If you want to have the power in this group, you should show them who the boss is first. Therefore, they will listen to you.

如果你想在这个团队中有影响力，你必须让他们知道谁才是做决定的人。如此，他们才会听你的。

work your fingers to the bone 　卖力工作

I will work my fingers to the bone for you.

我会为你卖力工作。

Unit 14 Go to a Hospital 医院

Daily Conversation 日常对话 | 模拟真实的日常对话

A Did you eat anything that was not fresh yesterday?
你昨天吃了什么不新鲜的食物吗？

B Well, I couldn't recall having eaten anything that was not fresh. Besides, I have a fever up to 38 ℃.
嗯，我实在想不起来吃了什么不新鲜的东西。还有，我现在发烧到38℃了。

A Let me take your temperature. I will use my <mark>stethoscope</mark> to check the sound of your heart beat and breath.
让我量一下你的体温。我将用我的听诊器听听你的心跳和呼吸的声音。

B Doctor, will I need to stay here and have my health checkup?
医生，我要在这里做健康检查吗？

A I will <mark>prescribe</mark> you some medicine first. If the pain still doesn't go away today, I am afraid you will have to come back and have your health checked.
我会先给你一些药，如果今天疼痛还是没有减轻的话，我想你恐怕要再回来做健康检查。

Additional Vocabulary & Phrases | 补充单词 & 短语

- **stethoscope** [n] 听诊器
  Almost every doctor needs a stethoscope.
  几乎每个医生都需要一个听诊器。

- **prescribe** [v] 为……开药方、开医嘱
  The doctor prescribed me some pain killer.
  医生给我开了一些止痛药。

Daily Sentences 高频用句 | 一分钟学一句，不怕不够用

- Can I make an appointment with Dr. Chen?
  我可以和陈医生预约吗？

- Can I take your **blood pressure** *1?
  我可以量你的血压吗？

- Let me measure your height and weight.
  让我量一下你的身高和体重。

- The doctor prescribed me some **medicine** *2.
  医生给我开了一些药。

- I have a headache, a stomachache, a runny nose, a stuffy nose and a fever.
  我头痛、胃痛、流鼻涕、鼻塞和发烧。

- I do not feel well and I feel dizzy all the time.
  我不太舒服而且一直头晕。

- I have a sore throat and my muscles are sore.
  我喉咙痛，还有我肌肉也酸痛。

- Did you eat anything that was not fresh yesterday? Or do you think your symptom are more like a cold?
  你昨天有吃什么不新鲜的食物吗？或者你觉得你的症状比较像感冒？

★ 换个单词说说看 | 用单词丰富句子，让句子更漂亮！

Additional Vocabulary & Phrases | 补充单词 & 短语

- **measure** v 测量
  We measured the length of the wall.
  我们测量了那面墙的长度。

- **dizzy** a 头晕目眩的
  I felt very dizzy.
  我感觉头晕目眩。

- **sore** a 酸痛的
  My arms are really sore.
  我的手臂很酸痛。

- **symptom** n 症状
  What are the symptoms of lung cancer?
  肺癌会有什么症状？

Daily Vocabulary 语言学校都会教的实用日常单词

1 hospital 医院

ward [wɔːd] [n]		病房
emergency room [ph]		急诊室
ambulance [ˈæmbjələns] [n]		救护车
pharmacy [ˈfɑːməsi] [n]		药店

2 patient 病人

fever [ˈfiːvə] [n]		发烧
cough [kɒf] [n]		咳嗽
cold [kəʊld] [n]		感冒
dizzy [ˈdɪzi] [a]		头晕
stomachache [ˈstʌməkeɪk] [n]		胃痛

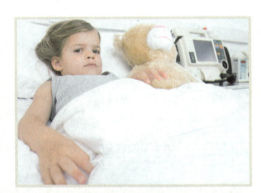

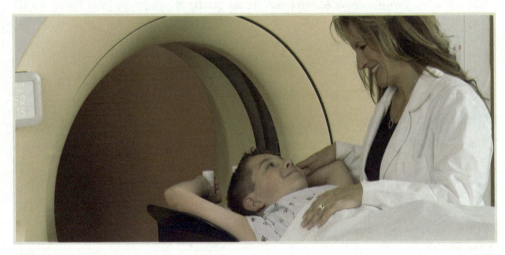

3 cancer 癌症

tumor [ˈtjuːmə] [n]	肿瘤	**ache** [eɪk] [v]		疼痛
chemotherapy [ˌkiːməʊˈθerəpi] [n]	化疗	**pulse** [pʌls] [n]		脉搏
diagnose [ˈdaɪəgnəʊz] [v]	诊断			

4 doctor 医生

dentist ['dentɪst] [n]	牙医
pediatrician [ˌpiːdiə'trɪʃn] [n]	儿科医师
obstetrician [ˌɒbstə'trɪʃn] [n]	妇产医师
ophthalmologist [ˌɒfθæl'mɒlədʒɪst] [n]	眼科医师
internist [ɪn'tɜːnɪst] [n]	内科医师
surgeon ['sɜːdʒən] [n]	外科医师

5 operating room 手术室

tweezers ['twiːzəz] [n]	镊子
face mask [ph]	口罩
syringe [sɪ'rɪndʒ] [n]	针筒
cotton ball [ph]	棉球
blood transfusion [ph]	输血
bandage ['bændɪdʒ] [n]	纱布

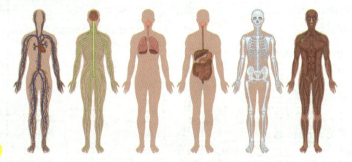

6 body 身体

head [hed] [n]	头
chest [tʃest] [n]	胸部
abdomen ['æbdəmən] [n]	腹部
heart [hɑːt] [n]	心脏
stomach ['stʌmək] [n]	胃
intestines [ɪn'testɪn] [n]	肠
liver ['lɪvə] [n]	肝
lung [lʌŋ] [n]	肺

7 pill 药丸

tablet ['tæblət] [n] —— 药片
dragee ['drɑːʒeɪ] [n] —— 糖衣丸
capsule ['kæpsjuːl] [n] —— 胶囊
eye drops [ph] —— 眼药水
cough syrup [ph] —— 咳嗽糖浆

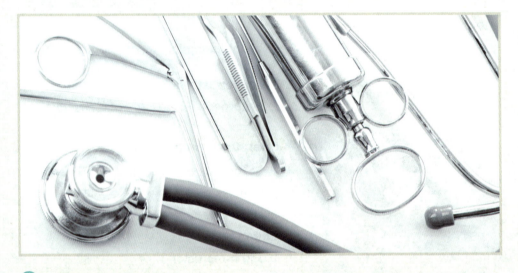

8 medical 医学的、医术的、医疗的

stretcher ['stretʃə] [n] —— 担架
crutch [krʌtʃ] [n] —— 拐杖
ear thermometer [ph] —— 耳温枪
sling [slɪŋ] [n] —— 三角巾
stethoscope ['steθəskəʊp] [n] —— 听诊器

Daily Q&A

〔会话一〕
Q▶ What symptoms do you have?
你有什么症状？
A▶ I have a sore throat.
我喉咙痛。

〔会话二〕
Q▶ Do you have a headache or a cold?
你头痛还是感冒？
A▶ I have a headache.
我头痛。

〔会话三〕
Q▶ Can I take your temperature?
我可以量你的体温吗？
A▶ Absolutely!
当然！

Proverbs & Idioms 地道谚语与惯用语 ｜ 让句子锦上添花

an apple a day keeps the doctor away　一天一颗苹果，医生远离你
If you want to prevent yourself from getting a bad cold, always remember that "an apple a day keeps the doctor away."
如果你想避免得重感冒，你一定要记得"一天一颗苹果，医生远离你"。

a spin doctor　统筹决策的人、军师
He needs a good spin doctor to help him win the election.
他需要一个好军师来帮他赢得选战。

doctor someone up　快速救治
That man is seriously injured. Give me a minute to doctor him up, and then we can send him to the hospital.
那个男人受伤很严重，让我帮他急救一下，然后再把他送到医院。

just what the doctor ordered　所期望并想要的事
An evening with lots of surprises is not just what the doctor ordered.
一个晚上发生这么多出乎意料的事，实在不是人想要的。

doctor's orders　医生的命令
I have to be on a vegetable diet. That is doctor's orders and I don't like it.
我只能吃蔬菜。这是医生的命令，但是我不喜欢。

a bitter pill to swallow　不能不做的苦差事、不得不忍受的屈辱
Losing the championship was a bitter pill to swallow for Jim who was used to winning every year.
对每年会赢的吉姆而言，失去冠军头衔是不得不忍受的屈辱。

do drugs　吸毒
Sam doesn't do drugs, and he doesn't drink.
山姆不吸毒也不喝酒。

rush someone to the hospital　把某人快速送到医院
We rushed him to the hospital after he complained of a serious chest pain.
他痛苦地说他胸很痛之后，我们快速地将他送到医院。

a clean bill of health　身体健康
Johnson was given a clean bill of health by his doctors in the beginning of this month.
强森这个月初被医生告知身体健康。

Unit 15 Go to the Bank 银行

Daily Conversation 日常对话 | 模拟真实的日常对话

A Hi, Jenny. You look like you are in a hurry to go somewhere. Where are you going?
嗨，珍妮。你看起来好像赶着去某处一样。你要去哪里？

B I am going to the bank. I need to cash some checks.
我要去银行。我要将支票兑换成现金。

A That's great. We can go to the bank together.
那太好了！我们可以一起去银行。

B Why are you going there? 为什么你要去那里？

A I will go to Japan on business for five days next Tuesday. I want to exchange some Japanese yen.
我下星期二会去日本出差五天。我想换一些日元。

B I see. Will you bring a lot of money with you? 我了解了。你会带很多钱去吗？

A Not really. I plan to bring some cash and withdraw money at the ATM in Japan. 不会。我计划带点现金，到日本再用取款机取钱。

Additional Vocabulary & Phrases | 补充单词 & 短语

- **in a hurry** [ph] 匆忙地
  She ate in a hurry.
  她匆忙地吃完东西。

- **exchange** [v] 交换、兑换
  I'd like to exchange some Thai bahts for dollars.
  我想要用些泰铢兑换美金。

- **plan** [v] 计划、打算
  I plan to go to New York next week.
  我计划下星期去纽约。

- **withdraw** [v] 抽回、提取
  Mom withdrew some money at the bank.
  妈妈在银行取了一些钱。

Daily Sentences | 高频用句 | 一分钟学一句，不怕不够用

- To open an account, you need a personal stamp, your **identification** card and some money.
  开一个账户，你需要印章、身份证和一些钱。

- Do you want to apply for a Visa or Master card?
  你想申请 Visa 或 Master 卡吗？

- To apply for a credit card, you need to have a copy of the bank statement which lists your **income** for the last three months.
  申请一张信用卡需要有一份你最近三个月的收入证明。

- I would like to rent a safe in your bank to store some of my **valuable** things.
  我想在你们银行租一个保险箱来存放我的贵重物品。

- I want to buy a house. I need to apply for a mortgage.
  我想买一栋房子。我想申请贷款。

- Can I **transfer** money to my son's account in Japan?
  我可以汇款到我儿子日本的账户吗？

- What is the US dollar to **RMB***1 exchange rate now?
  现在一美金可以兑换多少人民币？

- The security guard is paying full attention to the cash in the armored truck.
  这位警卫正全神贯注在这辆运钞车上。

- Do you have a **bank card***2 in Japan?
  你在日本有银行卡吗？

★ 换个单词说说看 | 用单词丰富句子，让句子更漂亮！

New Taiwan dollars*1 可以替换：

euro	Korean Won	Philippine Peso
欧元	韩元	菲律宾比索

What is the US dollar to _____ exchange rate now?
现在一美金兑换_____是多少？

bank card*2 可以替换：

debit card	credit card	loyalty card
现金卡	信用卡	积分卡

Do you a _____ in Japan?
你在日本有_____吗？

Additional Vocabulary & Phrases | 补充单词 & 短语

- identification [n] 身份证明、认出
  She uses her health insurance card as identification.
  她用医保卡当作身份证明。

- income [n] 收入、所得
  She doesn't have any income.
  她没有任何收入。

- valuable [a] 有价值的、值钱的
  This vase is really valuable.
  这个花瓶非常值钱。

- transfer [v] 转换、调动、改变
  Judi was transferred to a better school.
  茱蒂转到另一所更好的学校了。

Daily Vocabulary 语言学校都会教的实用日常单词

① counter 柜台、柜台式长桌

- **teller** ['telə] n. ——— 银行行员
- **cashier** [kæ'ʃɪə] n. ——— 出纳员
- **manager** ['mænɪdʒə] n. ——— 银行经理
- **security guard** ph. ——— 警卫
- **customer** ['kʌstəmə] n. ——— 顾客

② bill 汇票、单据

- **cash** [kæʃ] n. 现金 v. 把……兑现
- **currency exchange** ph. ——— 兑换货币
- **fund** [fʌnd] n. ——— 资金
- **check** [tʃek] n. ——— 支票（美国）

③ account 账户、客户

- **account** [ə'kaʊnt] n. ——— 现金账户
- **deposit** [dɪ'pɒzɪt] v. ——— 存钱
- **credit** ['kredɪt] 银行存款（账户余额）
- **currency** ['kʌrənsi] n. ——— 流通货币
- **check book** ph. ——— 支票本

④ credit card 信用卡

personal stamp [ph] ······ 图章、私章
identification card [ph] ······ 身份证
National Health Insurance Card [ph] ······ 医保卡

automatic teller machine [ph] ······ ATM 自动柜员机
bank card [ph] ······ 银行卡

⑤ business 事务

withdraw [wɪðˈdrɔː] [v] ······ 提款
savings [ˈseɪvɪŋz] [n] ······ 储蓄存款
borrow [ˈbɒrəʊ] [v] ······ 借款
loan [ləʊn] [n] ······ 贷款
transfer [trænsˈfɜː] [v] ······ 汇款

⑥ savings and loan association 信用合作社

interest [ˈɪntrəst] [n] ······ 利息、股份、股权
mortgage [ˈmɔːgɪdʒ] [n] ······ 抵押契据、抵押借款
save [seɪv] [v] ······ 储存
pay into [ph] ······ 把（钱）存银行
stock [stɒk] [n] ······ 股票、国债（英）
share [ʃeə] [n] ······ 股票、股份

7 vault 金库、保管库

alarm [əˈlɑːm] n ———— 警报器
safe [seɪf] n ———— 保险箱
safe-deposit box ph ———— 保险柜
surveillance camera ph ———— 监视器
coin [kɔɪn] n ———— 硬币
armored truck ph ———— 运钞车

8 commercial bank 商业银行

industrial development bank ph
———— 工业开发银行
federal bank ph ———— 联邦银行
mortgage bank ph ———— 抵押银行
land development's bank ph
———— 国土发展银行

indigenous bank ph ———— 国家银行
saving bank ph ———— 储蓄银行
exchange bank ph ———— 外汇银行
internet bank ph ———— 网上银行
offshore bank ph ———— 境外金融银行

Daily Q&A

〔会话一〕
Q▶ Can I open an saving account?
我可以开一个存款账户吗?
A▶ Sure. Please fill out the form first.
当然。请先把表格填好。

〔会话二〕
Q▶ How much money would you like to save for the first time?
你第一次想存多少钱?
A▶ I would like to save about 2,000 dollars.
我想存大约 2 000 美元。

〔会话三〕
Q▶ Do you also want to take out money with a bank card?
你想用银行卡取一些钱吗?
A▶ Yes, please.
是,麻烦你。

Proverbs & Idioms 地道谚语与惯用语 | 让句子锦上添花

break the bank　用完所有的钱
Buying a new pair of shoes at a discount price won't break the bank.
用折扣后的价格买一双鞋不会用完所有的钱。

bank on something　信赖某事
I'll pay back all the money. You can bank on me.
我会还清所有钱。你可以相信我。

laugh all the way to the bank　对已赚取的钱感到高兴
He may not be the greatest singer, but he is popular and can laugh all the way to the bank.
他可能不是最棒的歌手，但是他很受欢迎并且很满意自己赚得的钱。

cry all the way to the bank　对已赚取的钱感到失望
The movie sucks. Many people feel disappointed after seeing it. I think people who make the movie are crying all the way to the bank.
这部电影很烂。很多人在看过电影之后感到失望。我认为制作这部电影的人会对自己赚取的钱感到失望。

can take it to the bank　可以证明所说的是真的
What I am telling you is the truth. You can take it to the bank.
我所说的都是真的。你可以去求证。

be broke　没钱、穷光蛋
Jack is broke. He can't even afford to buy a cup of coffee.
杰克是个穷光蛋。他甚至买不起一杯咖啡。

a loan shark　放高利贷的人
That man was beaten because he was late to pay money back to a loan shark.
那个男人被打是因为他延迟还钱给放高利贷的人。

be strapped (for cash)　缺钱
I seem to be a bit strapped. Can you lend me some money?
我好像有点缺钱。你可以借我一些钱吗？

Unit 16 Go to a Post Office 邮局

Daily Conversation | 日常对话 | 模拟真实的日常对话

A Excuse me, Ma'am. I would like to mail this package door to door via air mail to London. It is a very important package and has to be sent within three days.
不好意思，小姐。我想用航空挂号邮寄这件包裹到伦敦。这是一个很重要的包裹，必须于三天内寄到。

B No problem. But the postage is much higher than that for a the regular package.
没问题。但是邮资会比一般的包裹贵很多。

A That's fine with me. I am willing to pay for it as long as you can guarantee me the package can arrive in time.
那没关系。我很愿意支付，只要你保证我的包裹可以准时寄到。

B OK. All the registered air mail packages will be received in 5 working days.
好的。所有的挂号航空包裹可在五个工作日内寄达。

A I see. How much do I need to pay in total for this package?
我知道了。这件包裹总共需要多少邮资？

B It's 500 dollars.
共 500 美元。

Additional Vocabulary & Phrases | 补充单词 & 短语

- **via** v 经由、透过
Jonathan flew to America via Thailand.
乔纳森经过泰国飞到美国。

- **guarantee** v 保证、担保
Cynthia guaranteed me this product is organic.
辛西亚向我保证这个产品是有机的。

Daily Sentences 高频用句 | 一分钟学一句，不怕不够用
03-14

- Excuse me. I would like to send this letter by air mail.
  不好意思，我想寄封航空信件。

- Excuse me. Can I send the file by **express** *1?
  不好意思。我可以用快递寄送这份文件吗？

- Please put the file in this paper box and **seal** it.
  请将文件放入纸盒里，并把盒子封好。

- How much is it to mail a **registered** package?
  寄一个挂号包裹要多少钱？

- I am collecting **postcards** *2.
  我正在收集明信片。

- You can buy a set of commemorative postcards **published** by the post office. They just came out last week.
  你可以买一套邮局发行的纪念明信片。它们上星期才发行。

- Where do I put the sender's and the receiver's address?
  我要在哪里填写寄件人和收件人的地址？

- How many days does it take to send a letter to Japan by surface mail?
  海运邮件到日本要多少天？

- What you need to do is to put a stamp with enough postage and **mark** the cover with "By Air Mail".
  你只要贴足够的邮资，并在上面注明"航空邮件"即可。

★ 换个单词说说看 | 用单词丰富句子，让句子更漂亮！

express *1 可以替换：

| Express 快递 | sea mail 海运 | prompt delivery mail 限时邮件 |

Can I deliver the file by _____?
我可以用_____寄送这份文件吗？

postcards *2 可以替换：

| stamps 邮票 | commemorative stamps 纪念邮票 | postmarked stamps 盖邮戳的邮票 |

I am collecting _____.
我在收集_____。

Additional Vocabulary & Phrases | 补充单词 & 短语

- **seal** [v] 密封
  Please seal this envelope.
  请将这个信封密封好。

- **register** [v] 登记、注册
  Have you registered for the piano class?
  你登记要上钢琴课了吗？

- **publish** [v] 发行、出版
  This book will be published next month.
  这本书将在下个月发行。

- **mark** [v] 做记号、记下
  Can you mark an "X" here in the corner?
  你能在角落这边记下一个"X"的记号吗？

Daily Vocabulary 语言学校都会教的实用日常单词

1 mailman 邮差

mail [meɪl] n	邮件
express [ɪk'spres] n	快递
mailbox ['meɪlbɒks] n	邮筒、私人信箱
postbox ['pəʊstbɒks] n	邮箱
deliver [dɪ'lɪvə] v	投递

2 package 包裹

postage ['pəʊstɪdʒ] n	邮资
international parcel ph	国际包裹
EMS (Express Mail Service) ph	邮政特快专递
prompt delivery mail ph	限时邮件
value-declared mail ph	保值邮件

3 address 地址

zip code ph	邮政编号
return address ph	寄件人地址
recipient's address ph	收件人地址
revenue stamp ph	印花税票
zone [zəʊn] n	区域

④ postmark 邮戳

commemorative stamp [ph]	纪念邮票
stamp [stæmp] [n]	邮票
stamp tax [ph]	印花税
canceled stamp [ph]	盖销票
stamp machine [ph]	打印机

⑤ postal 邮政的

postal clerk [ph]	邮政办事员
postal money order [ph]	（邮）汇票
insurance [ɪnˈʃʊərəns] [n]	保险
post office box [ph]	邮政专用信箱

⑥ letter 信件

personal mail [ph]	私人信件
air mail [ph]	航空邮件
surface mail [ph]	海运
registered letter [ph]	挂号信
printed material [ph]	印刷品

7 envelope 信封

letter paper [ph] ················· 信纸
post card [ph] ················· 明信片
box [bɑks] [n] ················· 纸箱
letterhead ['letəhed] [n] ······ 印在信纸的信头
bulk mail [ph] ················· 大宗函件

8 postal savings 邮政储金

remittances [rɪ'mɪtns] [n] ········ 汇款
life insurance [ph] ············ 人寿保险
agency services [ph] ·········· 代理

postal account withdrawal [ph] 划拨提款
financial calculator [ph] ········ 理财试算

Daily Q&A

〔会话一〕
Q▶ Where can I buy commemorative stamps?
哪里可以买到纪念邮票呢？
A▶ Go to counter No. 12, please.
请到第 12 号柜台。

〔会话二〕
Q▶ Can I apply for a personal mail box at the post office?
我可以申请一个邮局的私人信箱吗？
A▶ Sure!
可以！

〔会话三〕
Q▶ I need 3 postcards.
我需要三张明信片。
A▶ OK! They cost 30 dollars.
好的，总共 30 美元。

Proverbs & Idioms 地道谚语与惯用语 | 让句子锦上添花

snail mail 纸笔信件，用以区分电子邮件

It is outdated to send snail mails. Almost all the people send emails nowadays.
邮寄信件已过时了，大部分人现在都发送电子邮件。

junk mail 垃圾邮件

It seems to be unlikely not to receive any junk mail when you check your email. What you can do is to delete it with patience.
当你收电子邮件时，没有垃圾邮件似乎是不太可能的事。你能做的是有耐心地把它删掉。

by return mail 以回函方式

Since the bill is overdue, would you please send us your check back by return mail?
由于这张账单过期未缴，能否请你用回函寄回你的支票呢？

best things come in small packages 麻雀虽小，五脏俱全

Jenny always hates to be so short and tiny. However, her mother always says to her that best things come in small packages.
珍妮很讨厌自己又矮又小，但是她妈妈总是告诉她，麻雀虽小，五脏俱全。

a dear John letter 分手信

Susan doesn't love her boyfriend any more. She plans to send him a dear John letter.
苏珊不再爱她的男朋友了，她计划写封分手信给他。

bread and butter letters 感谢信

Karen just had the meeting with Mr. and Mrs. Brown. After she went back to the office, she spent some time writing bread and butter letters to them.
凯伦刚刚和伯朗夫妇开会。回到公司后，她花了一些时间写感谢信给他们。

go postal 抓狂、变得超级生气

My boyfriend will go postal if he sees me hang out with Jason.
我男朋友如果看到我和杰森出去会抓狂。

Everyday Sentences　语言学校独家传授的必备好句子

- You put the sender's address on the top left corner, and the receiver's address in the center.
  你要在左上角写寄件人的住址，并在中间写收件人住址。

- Read the note carefully and follow the steps on the note. I am sure you can retrieve your letter.
  仔细阅读通知并遵照上面的步骤。我想你一定可以收到你的信。

- The postage depends on the weight of the package. The more it weighs, the more you pay.
  邮资要视包裹重量而定。重量越重价格就越贵。

- I missed an important letter when I went out this afternoon. All I have is a note left by the postman.
  我今天下午出门时错过了一封重要邮件。我只收到邮差留下的一个通知。

- Do I need to include my zip code in the address?
  需要在住址中加上我的邮政编码吗？

- Thank you very much. Here is 500 dollars.
  非常感谢你。这是 500 美元。

- Here is your receipt. Contact us if your friend still doesn't receive the package after 5 work days.
  这是你的收据。如果你的朋友在五个工作日后没收到包裹的话，可联系我们。

- You had better include the zip code on the letter because it is easier for the mailman to find the correct mailing place.
  最好加上邮政编码，这样邮差较易找到正确的邮寄地址。

- How may I help you?
  我能为你服务吗？

- What do you recommend?
  你有什么建议呢？

MEMO

From AM-PM 从早到晚都用得到的必备好句子

- I can mop the floor.
  我可以拖地。

- I can sweep the floor.
  我可以扫地。

- I need to prepare my lunchbox for tomorrow.
  我得准备明天的便当。

- It is time to start preparing to go to bed.
  该准备上床了。

- Hang up the phone and get into bed.
  挂掉电话去睡觉。

- We're not allowed to have guests over after 12 am.
  我们晚上12点后禁止会客。

- I'm tired.
  我好累。

- If you finish your homework, you can watch TV for one hour.
  如果你功课做完了，你可以看一小时电视。

- May I use the computer?
  我可以用电脑吗？

- You are allowed to use the computer after finishing your homework.
  你写完功课之后可以使用电脑。

- I can't sleep!
  我睡不着！

MEMO

- I want to sleep, but I can't.
  我很想睡，但睡不着。

- Do you have any suggestions for my insomnia?
  对于我的失眠问题，你有什么建议吗？

- I'm really a bad singer.
  我唱歌很难听。

- Don't worry. KTV is just a place to relax and have fun.
  不要担心！KTV 只是个让你放松、快乐的地方。

- I love singing!
  我喜欢唱歌！

- Shilin night market has some of the best food stands in Taipei.
  士林夜市有台北最棒的小吃摊。

- You can buy pearl milk tea at this drink stand.
  你可以在这饮料摊买珍珠奶茶。

- How do you eat chicken feet?
  鸡爪要怎么吃？

- I love trying all types of snacks.
  我喜欢尝试各种不同的小吃。

- I don't know what to get for him.
  我不知道要买什么给他。

- I hope he likes this present.
  我希望他喜欢这份礼物。

MEMO

Chapter 4

Exercising
运动身体好

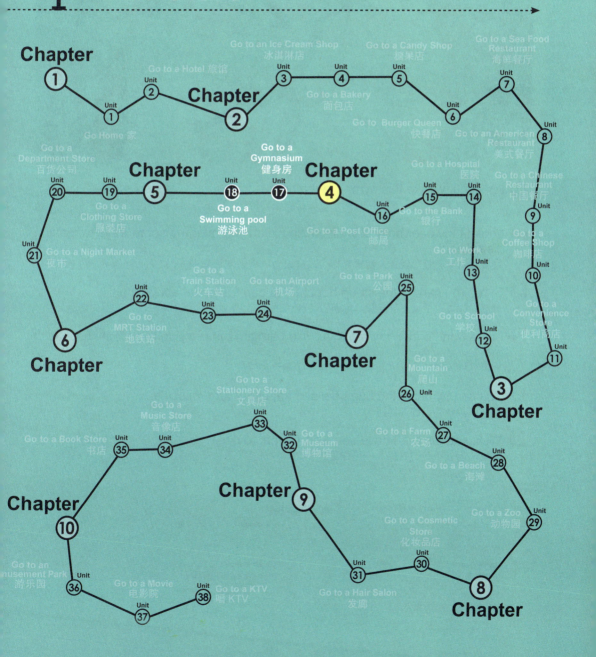

Unit 17 Go to a Gymnasium 健身房

Daily Conversation 日常对话 | 模拟真实的日常对话

A I bet you will like this gym. It is the best in town.
我打赌你会喜欢的,这家健身房是这城市中最好的。

B Look at my beer **belly**. It is **disgusting**. Can you offer me some ways to make it **disappear**?
看看我的啤酒肚,真令人讨厌!你可以建议我一些方法让它消失吗?

A Sure. You can try the sit-up bench. You can train your **abdominals**.
当然,你可以试试仰卧起坐。你可以训练你的腹部。

B I also want to train my arms. It's like I am always carrying two meaty bags with me.
我也想训练我的手臂。我看起来好像挂了两个肉袋。

A You can try using the dumbbells to train your arm muscles.
你可以用哑铃训练你的肌肉。

B Well, sounds like I have some hard work to do.
好吧,听起来我还有好长一段路要走。

Additional Vocabulary & Phrases | 补充单词 & 短语

- **belly** n 肚子
  Sherri has a big belly.
  雪莉有一个大肚子。

- **disgusting** a 令人作呕的、十分讨厌的
  The dirty warehouse is really disgusting.
  那个肮脏的仓库真的很恶心。

- **disappear** v 消失、不见
  The magician made the bird disappear.
  魔术师把小鸟变没了。

- **abdominals** n 腹部、腹肌
  I want to train my abdominals.
  我想训练我的腹肌。

Daily Sentences 高频用句 | 一分钟学一句，不怕不够用 04-02

- How can I become your member?
  要如何才能成为你们的会员呢？

- If I want to train my thighs and back, what equipment should I use?
  如果我想训练我的大腿和背肌，要用什么器材呢？

- What facilities do you have?
  你们有什么设备？

- Can I hire a personal coach to teach me how to train my abdominals?
  我可以请一个私人教练教我训练我的腹部吗？

- You can ask for more information at the information desk.
  你可以在询问处询问更多的相关信息。

- How much do I need to pay for a membership for one year?
  我要为一年会员资格付多少钱？

- When is the yoga*1 class?
  瑜伽课是什么时候？

- Excuse me, can you show me how to use the pedometer*2?
  不好意思，你可以使用计步器给我看吗？

- You can use the treadmill and the back extension bench over there.
  你可以使用那边的跑步机和背部伸展机。

★ 换个单词说说看 | 用单词丰富句子，让句子更漂亮！

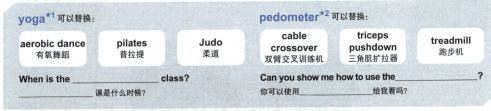

Additional Vocabulary & Phrases | 补充单词 & 短语

- **train** [v] 训练、培养
  Cynthia was trained to be an excellent nurse.
  辛西亚被培养成一个优秀的护士。

- **hire** [v] 雇用
  We need to hire another assistant.
  我们需要雇用另一个助手。

- **personal** [a] 个人的、私人的
  This is my personal notebook.
  这是我私人的笔记本。

- **extension** [n] 伸展、身长
  We asked our professor for a two-day extension to the final report.
  我们请求教授期末报告再给我们延长两天。

Daily Vocabulary 语言学校都会教的实用日常单词
04-03

1 fitness 健康

yoga ['jəʊgə] [n]		瑜伽
aerobic dance [ph]		有氧舞蹈
pilates [n]		普拉提
boxing ['bɒksɪŋ] [n]		拳击
Judo ['dʒuːdəʊ] [n]		柔道

2 kinesiology 人体运动学

coach [kəʊtʃ] [n]		教练
shape up [ph]		减肥
training ['treɪnɪŋ] [n]		训练、锻炼
goal [gəʊl] [n]		目标
energy ['enədʒi] [n]		活力、精力

3 gloves 拳击手套

wraps [ræpz] [n]	护腕		towel ['taʊəl] [n]	毛巾
weightlifting belt [ph]	举重带		sneaker ['sniːkə] [n]	运动鞋
wrist straps [ph]	手腕带			

4 energy drink 能量饮料

mineral water [ph]		矿泉水
bottled water [ph]		瓶装水
vitamin [ˈvɪtəmɪn] [n]		维生素
electrolyte [ɪˈlektrəlaɪt] [n]		电解质

5 muscle 肌、肌肉

biceps [ˈbaɪseps] [n]	二头肌	chest [tʃest] [n]	胸大肌
triceps [ˈtraɪseps] [n]	三头肌	abdominals [æbˈdɒmɪnlz] [n]	腹肌
shoulders [ˈʃəʊldə] [n]	三角肌	thighs [θaɪz] [n]	腿肌
traps [træpz] [n]	斜方肌	back [bæk] [n]	背肌

6 sauna 蒸汽浴、桑拿浴

steam sauna chamber [ph]	蒸气室
sauna cabinet [ph]	烤箱
infrared ray radiation sauna [ph]	红外线烤箱
jacuzzi [dʒəˈkuːzi] [n]	按摩浴池
massage chair [ph]	按摩椅
locker [ˈlɒkə] [n]	置物柜

7 cycling 骑脚踏车

dancing [ˈdɑːnsɪŋ] [n] .... 跳舞
ice-skating [ph] .... 溜冰
hiking [ˈhaɪkɪŋ] [n] .... 徒步旅行
skiing [ˈskiːɪŋ] [n] .... 滑雪
hockey [ˈhɒki] [n] .... 冰球

8 gymnasium 体育馆、健身房

back extension bench [ph] 背部伸展机
cable crossover [ph] 双臂交叉训练机
climber [ˈklaɪmə] 登山踏步机
dumbbell [ˈdʌmbel] [n] 哑铃
pedometer [peˈdɒmɪtə] [n] 计步器
recumbent bike [ph] 斜式健身车

Roman chair [ph] .... 罗马椅训练机
rotary torso [ph] .... 转体机
seated row [ph] .... 坐式划船器
sit-up bench [ph] .... 仰卧起坐台
stepper [ˈstepə] [n] .... 踏步机
triceps pushdown [ph] .... 三角肌扩拉器
treadmill [n] .... 跑步机

Daily Q&A

〔会话一〕
Q▶ Can I have the timetable of the dance classes of your gym?
我可以要一张你们健身房舞蹈课程的时刻表吗?

A▶ Sure. There you go.
当然,在这里。

〔会话二〕
Q▶ Where is the jacuzzi?
按摩浴缸在哪里?

A▶ Go ahead to the end and turn left.
直走到底左转。

〔会话三〕
Q▶ Where can I put my bags?
我可以把袋子放在哪里呢?

A▶ You can put your bags in the locker.
你可以把包放入置物柜里。

Proverbs & Idioms 地道谚语与惯用语 | 让句子锦上添花

muscle (someone) out of (something) 迫使某人不参与某事
Tommy tries to muscle Jack out of the job because he doesn't like Jack's ideas.
汤米迫使杰克不参与这项工作，因为他不喜欢杰克的主意。

muscle in on (something) 强迫更换或占有别人的财产、感情或兴趣
Don't try to muscle in on my project. If you do, you will be facing big trouble.
不要试着强迫更换我的计划，如果你这样做的话，你会有大麻烦。

pull a muscle 肌肉拉伤
I pulled a muscle in my arm and can't play tennis today.
我拉伤了手臂的肌肉，今天没办法打网球了。

flex your muscles 用行动让对方知道自己的能力
This poor country began to flex its muscles as the biggest producer in wine industry.
这个贫穷国家以开始成为最大的酒品制造商的方式，让大家知道它的实力。

not move a muscle 保持不动
I am worn out. I can't move a muscle after climbing the mountains for a whole day.
我累死了。在爬了一整天的山之后，我动弹不得。

blind-sided 没看到
Tim blind-sided the ball was thrown across the field.
提姆没看到横跨球场丢来的球。

the ball is in your court 自己要做的决定或责任
Remember that the ball is in your court whenever you have doubts in life.
记得每当你生命有困惑时都要自己做决定。

Unit 18 Go to a Swimming Pool 游泳池

Daily Conversation 日常对话 | 模拟真实的日常对话

A I used to be on my school team when I was a high school student.
我还是高中生的时候，曾是校游泳队的。

B Wow, I never heard you mention about it. Do you know how to do the freestyle?
哇，我从来没听你提起过。你知道怎么游自由泳吗？

A Sure, it's easy. You just wave one of your arms to the front and the other one to the back and flip your two feet regularly in the water.
当然，非常简单。你只要将你其中的一只手臂往前划，另一只手臂往后划，并且规律地在水里用脚拍水就可以了。

B I see. I still need floats to help me stay on top of the water. I am so afraid of sinking.
我知道了。我还需要游泳圈让我浮在水面上，我真的很害怕沉下去。

A You should try to do it without using any floats. You can learn faster that way.
你应该试着不要用游泳圈游游看。这样会比较快学会。

B Let's jump into the water and start swimming now.
我们下水开始游吧。

Additional Vocabulary & Phrases | 补充单词 & 短语

- **mention** v 提到、说起
  Emily mentioned something about her friends.
  艾米莉提到一些关于她朋友的事情。

- **sink** v 下沉
  The stone sank into the water.
  石头沉到水里了。

Daily Sentences 高频用句 | 一分钟学一句，不怕不够用
MP3 04-05

- How many laps do you swim every time you go swimming?
  你每次游泳可以游几圈？

- Can you do the breaststroke*1?
  你会游蛙泳吗？

- When doing the breaststroke, you need to put your two arms in the front and bend your knees a bit and kick in the water.
  游蛙泳的时候，你只需要把两只手放在前面，并把膝盖弯曲在水中踢水就可以了。

- It's very dangerous to swim in the sea.
  在海里游泳很危险。

- What do I need to wear when I go swimming?
  我游泳的时候要穿什么？

- Do you know how to breathe properly when swimming?
  你知道在游泳时怎么正确换气吗？

- How can I apply for a membership at this swimming pool?
  我要怎么申请加入这个游泳池的会员？

- Remember to do some warm-up exercises before you swim.
  游泳前记得要做暖身运动。

- I can teach you how to dog paddle*2.
  我可以教你怎么游狗刨式。

★ 换个单词说说看 | 用单词丰富句子，让句子更漂亮！

Additional Vocabulary & Phrases | 补充单词 & 短语

- **bend** [v] 使弯曲，折弯
  Adonis was so strong that he could bend the metal bar.
  阿多尼斯强壮到可以把金属棍子折弯。

- **kick** [v] 踢
  Mom, He just kicked me!
  妈，他刚才踢我！

- **dangerous** [a] 危险的
  It's dangerous to walk alone at night.
  晚上独自一个人走是很危险的。

- **warm-up** [ph] 暖身
  It's important to do warm-up before doing exercise.
  运动前暖身是很重要的。

Daily Vocabulary 语言学校都会教的实用日常单词

1 swimsuit 泳装

swimming trunks [ph]	....	泳裤
swimming cap [ph]	....	泳帽
bikini [bɪˈkiːni] [n]	....	比基尼
goggles [ˈɡɒɡlz] [n]	....	泳镜
earplugs [ˈɪəplʌɡz] [n]	....	耳塞

2 breaststroke 蛙泳

freestyle [ˈfriːstaɪl] [n]	....	自由泳
backstroke [ˈbækstrəʊk] [n]	....	仰泳
butterfly stroke [ph]	....	蝶泳
dog paddle [ph]	....	狗刨
float [fləʊt] [a]	....	漂浮的

3 swimming pool 游泳池

poolside [ˈpuːlsaɪd] [a]	.... 游泳池边的		depth [depθ] [n]	.... 深度
hot tub [ph]	.... 热水池		lane [leɪn] [n]	.... 泳道
wave pool [ph]	.... 海浪池			

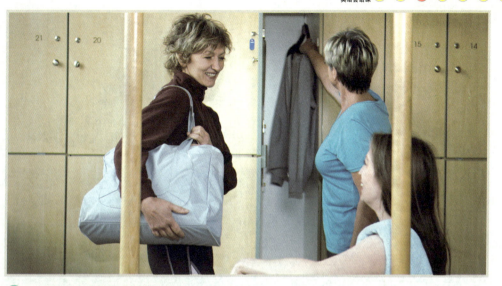

4 changing room 更衣室

shower [ˈʃaʊə] n	淋浴
get dressed ph	换装
dry off ph	擦干
locker room ph	置物柜间
spin dryer ph	脱水机

5 cannonball 抱膝跳水

diving [ˈdaɪvɪŋ] n	跳水
figure [ˈfɪgə] n	花式
belly flop ph	腹部先着水的跳水动作
shallow dive ph	浅潜
lap [læp] n	一圈（来回游泳池一趟）

6 lifeguard 救生员

ladder [ˈlædə] n	梯子
diving board ph	跳水板
lounge chair ph	躺椅
life ring ph	游泳圈
life jacket ph	救生衣

7 brush 梳子

sunscreen ['sʌnskriːn] [n] ……… 防晒乳
kickboard ['kɪkbɔːd] [n] ……… 浮板
waterproof bag [ph] ……… 防水包包
floaties [n] ……… 手套式游泳圈
swim fins [ph] ……… 脚蹼

8 profession 专业

Synchronized swimming [ph] 水上芭蕾
timekeeper ['taɪmkiːpə] [n]
　　　　　　　　　　（比赛中的）计时员
contestant [kən'testənt] [n] 竞争者
cardiopulmonary resuscitation [ph]
　　　　　　　　　　CPR 心肺复苏术

land drill [ph] ……… 陆上练习
long distance [ph] ……… 长距离游泳
middle distance [ph] ……… 中距离游泳
short distance [ph] ……… 短距离游泳
swimming committee [ph] ……… 游泳协会

Daily Q&A

〔会话一〕
Q▶ Do you know how to do the breaststroke?
你会游蛙泳吗？
A▶ No, I don't.
我不会。

〔会话二〕
Q▶ Can you help me put some sunscreen on?
你能帮我上点防晒乳吗？
A▶ Sure!
当然！

〔会话三〕
Q▶ Where are you going?
你要去哪里？
A▶ I'm going to the swimming pool.
我要去游泳池。

Proverbs & Idioms 地道谚语与惯用语 | 让句子锦上添花

sink or swim 沉或浮、成功或失败
Newcomers are given no training. They are simply left to sink or swim.
新来的人不会被训练，就让他们自生自灭吧。

swim against the tide 持相反意见
He always swims against the tide of public opinions.
他总是和大家持相反的意见。

swim in something 充满很多……
Every meal at my home swims in grease. How can I not become fatter?
我们家每次吃饭都吃得很油，我怎么能不变胖啊？

out of the swim of things 没有参与事务
I have been out of the swim of things for a few weeks. Please bring me up-to-date.
我已经好几周没有参与事务了，请告诉我最新的进度。

make someone's head swim 使困扰头晕
All the numbers make my head swim.
所有的数字都让我头晕。

still waters run deep 深藏不露、水深不可测
He's quiet and shy. But still waters run deep.
他很安静和害羞。但是这样的人是深藏不露的。

in deep water 危险的处境
Bill got in deep water in math class. The class is too difficult for him, and he's almost failing.
比尔在他的数学中里处境艰难。这堂课对他来说太难了，而且他快被挂了。

keep one's head above water 避开麻烦
Try to keep your head above water when there are economy crises.
有经济危机时你要试着避开麻烦。

pour cold water on something 浇冷水
John poured cold water on the whole project by refusing to participate.
约翰用拒绝加入来给整个计划浇冷水。

Everyday Sentences **语言学校独家传授必备好句子**

- Look at the water ballet dancers over there. They can do the figure stroke up and down the water.
  看那边的水上芭蕾舞演员，他们可以在水中做花式动作，游上又游下。

- I swim about twenty laps.
  我大约可以游 20 圈。

- You need to find a place where you see a lifeguard on the shore when swimming in the sea.
  在海里游泳时必须找一个可以看到岸边有救生员的地方。

- You need to wear a swimming cap, a swim suit, ear plugs and goggles when swimming.
  游泳的时候你要穿戴泳帽、泳衣、耳塞和泳镜。

- You should do CPR on the people who drown.
  你应该对溺水的人做心肺复苏术。

- When your leg cramps, you need to stretch it for a second until the feeling disappear.
  当你的腿抽筋时，你要把腿伸直一下，直到抽筋的感觉消失为止。

- Where can I put my clothes and bags at this swimming pool?
  在游泳池时，我可以把衣服和包包放在哪里？

- I have a swimming class this afternoon. Do you want to go with me?
  我今天下午有游泳课，你要一起来吗？

- I am getting fatter and fatter. I need to do some exercise to lose some weight.
  我越来越胖了，我需要运动一下来减肥。

- Can you swim? I am still learning how to breathe in the water.
  你会游泳吗？我还在学怎么在水中换气。

MEMO

From AM-PM 从早到晚都用得到的必备好句子

- This is the perfect present for him!
  这礼物最适合他了！

- What's your best offer?
  你能给的最好价格是多少？

- Can I get a special discount?
  我能有些优惠吗？

- Your price is outrageous!
  你的价钱太夸张了！

- These t-shirts are on sale.
  这些T恤在特价卖。

- All winter clothing is now 30% off.
  冬季服饰现在打7折。

- What's your size?
  你穿几号呢？

- Do you have this dress in size 8?
  你这件连衣裙有8号的吗？

- I'm afraid we don't have your size.
  我恐怕已经没有你的尺寸了。

- Would you like to see a movie tonight?
  你晚上要不要看电影？

- What movie do you want to watch?
  你想看哪一部电影？

MEMO

- What movies are in theater now?
  现在上映的电影有什么？

- What's your favorite clothing brand?
  你最喜欢哪个牌子的衣服呢？

- Which dress do you think I should buy?
  你觉得我该买哪一件连衣裙？

- I don't look good in stripes.
  我穿条纹不好看。

- What material is this T-shirt made of?
  这件 T 恤的材质是什么？

- I can't decide which shirt to buy.
  我没办法决定该买哪一件衬衫。

- What shade of lipstick matches my skin tone?
  哪种颜色的口红适合我的肤色？

- I want to try this blush on my cheeks.
  我想在脸颊上试擦这个腮红。

- How do I remove this make up?
  我该如何卸妆？

- Making yourself beautiful may cost a lot.
  让自己变美是很花钱的。

- How long do you spend putting make up on?
  你化妆要花多久时间啊？

MEMO

Chapter 5

Shopping
逛街好心情

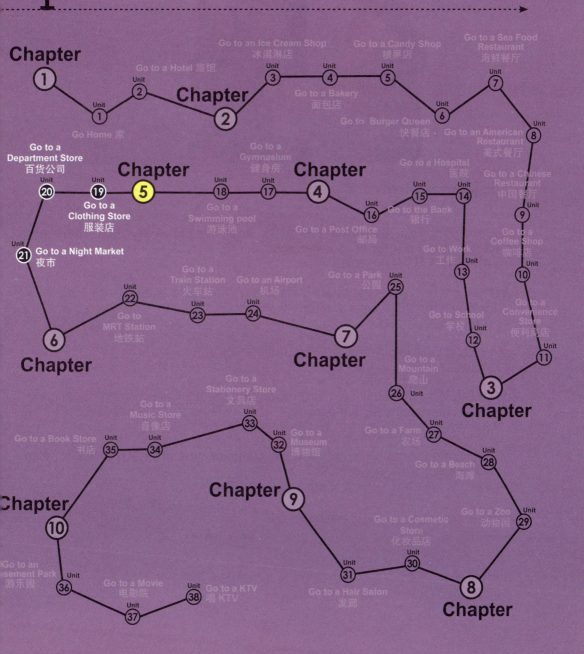

Unit 19 Go to a Clothing Store 服装店

Daily Conversation | 日常对话 | 模拟真实的日常对话

A Hmm, what should I wear today?
嗯，我今天要穿哪件衣服？

B Come on, you think about what to wear almost every day. There are thousands of clothes in your **wardrobe**.
拜托，你几乎每天都在想要穿哪件？你的衣柜里头有数以千计的衣服了。

A Well, haven't you ever heard people say that there is always one piece of clotheing missing from a women's wardrobe?
哎哟，你没听过人家说"女人的衣柜总是少一件衣服"吗？

B I do and I can **prove** that is 100 % true for you.
我知道，而且我可以从你身上百分之百证明是真的。

A Loving to look beautiful is women's **nature**. In fact, I am thinking about going to my favorite clothing shop today.
爱漂亮是女人的天性，事实上，我在想今天要去一间我最喜欢的服饰店。

B No kidding! Again?! You just went shopping yesterday. You really are a **shopaholic**.
别开玩笑了！又来了！你昨天才买了衣服，你真的是一个购物狂。

Additional Vocabulary & Phrases | 补充单词 & 短语

- **wardrobe** n 衣柜
  We have a wooden wardrobe in our room.
  我们有一个木衣柜在房间里。

- **prove** v 证明
  I'll prove you are wrong!
  我会证明你是错的！

- **nature** n 自然、天性
  I like to be close to nature.
  我喜欢接近大自然。

- **shopaholic** n 购物狂
  You are really a shopaholic.
  你真的是一个购物狂。

Daily Sentences 高频用句 | 一分钟学一句，不怕不够用

- Do you have this **shirt**★1 in a bigger size?
  你这件衬衫有大一号的吗？

- What other **colors**★2 does this T-shirt come in?
  这款 T 恤还有哪些颜色？

- When will you have a big **sale**?
  你们什么时候有大减价？

- Our store usually has a big sale in July and January. All the **prices** are up to 70% off.
  我们店通常在 7 月和 1 月的时候有大减价，所有的商品都打 3 折。

- How much does the bag cost after the **discount**?
  这个袋子打折后是多少钱？

- Can I try on these clothes?
  我可以试穿这些衣服吗？

- Does this scarf come in yellow?
  这条围巾有黄色的吗？

- Excuse me, the skirt is too **loose**. Do you have a smaller one?
  不好意思，这裙子太松了，你们有小一号的吗？

- I think the hat does not fit me. Do you have it in other styles?
  我想那个帽子不适合我，你们有其他款式的吗？

★ 换个单词说说看 | 用单词丰富句子，让句子更漂亮！

Additional Vocabulary & Phrases | 补充单词 & 短语

- **sale** [n] 卖、拍卖
  They have a garage sale tomorrow.
  他们明天会有一个旧物拍卖。

- **price** [n] 价钱
  The price of the dress is too high.
  那件连衣裙的价钱太高了。

- **discount** [n] 折扣
  Can you give me some discount?
  你能给我打一些折扣吗？

- **loose** [a] 松的、宽的
  This pants is too loose.
  这件裤子太松了。

Daily Vocabulary 语言学校都会教的实用日常单词
05-03

1 catalogue 目录

clothes [kləʊðz] n	衣服
model ['mɒdl] n	模特
style [staɪl] n	款式
colorful ['kʌləfl] a	鲜艳的
simple ['sɪmpl] a	简单的
popular ['pɒpjələ] a	流行的
fashionable ['fæʃnəbl] a	时髦的
noble ['nəʊbl] a	高贵的

2 fitting room 试穿间

size [saɪz] n	尺寸
fitting ['fɪtɪŋ] n	试穿
wear [weə] v	穿、戴
fit [fɪt] v	（衣服）使……合身
coordinate [kəʊ'ɔːdɪneɪt] v	搭配

3 top 上衣

T-shirt ['tiːʃɜːt] n	T恤
dress [dres] n	连衣裙
shirt [ʃɜːt] n	衬衫
blouse [blaʊz] n	（妇女、儿童等的）短上衣、短衫
coat [kəʊt] n	外套、大衣
jumper ['dʒʌmpə] n	毛线衣、（背心连裤的）娃娃服
sweater ['swetə] n	毛衣
jacket ['dʒækɪt] n	夹克
tank top ph	无袖背心

④ pants 裤子、长裤

slacks [slæks] [n]		宽松的长裤
trousers ['traʊzəz] [n]		长裤
shorts [ʃɔːts] [n]		宽松运动短裤
jeans [dʒiːnz] [n]		牛仔裤
skirt [skɜːt] [n]		裙子
pantskirt [pæntskɜːt] [n]		裤裙

⑤ hat 帽子

baseball cap [ph]		棒球帽
balmoral [bæl'mɒrəl] [n]		苏格兰无边圆顶帽
beret ['bereɪ] [n]		贝雷帽
boonie hat [ph]		登山帽
fedora [fɪ'dɔːrə] [n]		绅士软呢帽
top hat [ph]		绅士高礼帽

⑥ scarf 围巾、领带

belt [belt] [n]	腰带	bow [baʊ] [n]		蝴蝶领结
necktie ['nektaɪ] [n]	领带、领结	neckerchief ['nekətʃiːf] [n]		领巾
sock [sɒk] [n]	袜子			

7 jewelry 首饰

earrings [ˈɪərɪŋ] n		耳环
ring [rɪŋ] n		戒指
necklace [ˈnekləs] n		项链
bracelet [ˈbreɪslət] n		手链
jewel [ˈdʒuːəl] n		宝石
accessory [əkˈsesəri] n		配件
trinket [ˈtrɪŋkɪt] n		小装饰物、廉价首饰
glasses [ɡlɑːs] n		眼镜

8 underwear 内衣

undergarment [ˈʌndəɡɑːmənt] n	内衣裤
briefs [briːfs] n	三角裤
panties [ˈpæntiz] n	内裤
thong [θɒŋ] n	丁字裤
bra [brɑː] n	胸罩
corset [ˈkɔːsɪt] n	马甲
front closure ph	前扣式胸罩
nursing bra ph	哺乳用胸罩
seamless bra ph	无痕内衣
sports bra ph	运动胸罩
bustier [ˈbʌstiə] n	调整型内衣

Daily Q&A

〔会话一〕
Q▶ How much are a blouse and a pair of pants in total?
一件女款上衣和一件裤子总共多少钱？
A▶ They are 3, 000 dollars.
它们总共是 3 000 美元。

〔会话二〕
Q▶ Good morning, sir. How can I help you?
早安，先生。我能为您效劳吗？
A▶ No, thanks. I am just browsing around.
不用，我只是到处看看。

〔会话三〕
Q▶ Where is the fitting room?
试衣间在哪里？
A▶ It is at the end of the aisle.
在走道的最后面。

Proverbs & Idioms 地道谚语与惯用语 | 让句子锦上添花

give someone the shirt off one's back 尽全力帮助别人
You can depend on Jack when you are in trouble. He would give you the shirt off his back.
你有麻烦的时候可以依靠杰克,他会尽全力地帮助你。

keep your shirt on! 等一下、耐心点
Keep your shirt on! I will be right back with you in a minute.
耐心点!我马上就回来。

lose one's shirt 输钱
I almost lost my shirt on that investment. Luckily, I also invested my money on some other things.
我几乎在那项投资里输掉所有的钱,但很幸运,我也投资一些别的东西。

wear several hats 身兼数职
Tina needs money. She now wears several hats to make her ends meet.
缇娜需要钱,她现在身兼数职赚取生活费。

I'll eat my hat if ... ……如果(一件不可能的事发生),我就把我的头剁下(帽子吃掉)
I'll eat my hat if the sun rises from the west.
如果太阳从西边出来,我就把我的头剁下来给你。

dress to the nines 穿着华丽、盛装
Lena dressed to the nines to the party. She wanted to impress her boyfriend.
莉娜衣着华丽出席派对。她想要让她的男朋友印象深刻。

keep something zipped 保守秘密
Will broke up with her girlfriend. He hasn't let anyone know. Let's keep the news zipped.
威尔和她的女朋友分手了。他还没让任何人知道。让我们先保守这个秘密。

Unit 20 Go to a Department Store 百货公司

Daily Conversation | 日常对话 | 模拟真实的日常对话

A Tiffany, look at the long line in front of the department store. I think they are having their **annual** sale again.
蒂芬妮，看看百货公司前面排队的那些人，我想百货公司的周年庆又到了。

B Really? Then, how can I miss such a great timing to buy some cheap facial **treatment** product.
真的吗？那我怎么能错失买便宜保养品的好时机呢？

A Are you sure? It's really **crowded** inside. I can **hardly** breathe every time I go there during the annual sales.
你确定？里面真的很挤。每次周年庆的时候我到那里几乎都没办法呼吸。

B But, everything is really on special discount.
但是，所有东西真的有特别的折扣。

A You are right. But, we had better look at the catalog and make a shopping list first. I do not want to waste my time.
对呀，但是我们最好先看一下目录，然后列一下购物清单，我不想浪费我的时间。

B That is a good idea.
这是个好主意。

Additional Vocabulary & Phrases | 补充单词 & 短语

- **annual** [a] 一年一次的、年度的
  Kevin's annual income is $ 3 million dollars.
  凯文的年收入是 300 万美元。

- **treatment** [n] 治疗、处理
  Dr. Wu suggested me trying a new treatment for my skin.
  吴医师建议我试试一个新的皮肤治疗。

- **crowded** [a] 拥挤的
  The new restaurant is always crowded.
  那家新的餐厅总是挤满很多人。

- **hardly** [a] 简直不、几乎不
  I can hardly eat anything today.
  我今天几乎吃不下任何东西。

Daily Sentences 高频用句 | 一分钟学一句，不怕不够用
05-05

- Alice, are you free to go to the department store with me this afternoon?
  艾丽丝，你今天下午有空跟我一起到百货公司吗？

- I need to buy some make-up.
  我需要买一些化妆品。

- Where is the information desk?
  询问处在哪里？

- The **shoe shop**[1] is in the center of the **ground floor**.
  鞋店在一楼中间。

- Which floor sells appliances?
  哪一层楼卖家电用品？

- The **new Italian restaurant**[1] is on the 10th floor.
  新的意大利餐厅在10楼。

- Do you **accept** credit cards?
  你们接受信用卡吗？

- Can I get a special discount?
  我可以要特别折扣吗？

- Is there a book store in this building?
  这栋楼有书店吗？

- Do you offer any free delivery service?
  你们提供免费送货的服务吗？

★ 换个单词说说看 | 用单词丰富句子，让句子更漂亮！

shoe shop[1] 可以替换：

| bag store 包店 | jewelry store 珠宝店 | bedding store 寝具店 |

The _____ is in the center of the ground floor.
_____ 在一楼中间。

new Italian restaurant[2] 可以替换：

| coffee shop 咖啡厅 | ice cream store 冰淇淋店 | food court 美食区 |

The _____ is on the 10th floor.
新的 _____ 在10楼。

Additional Vocabulary & Phrases | 补充单词 & 短语

- **ground floor** ph 一楼
  The ice cream shop is on the ground floor of the mall.
  冰淇淋店在购物商场的一楼。

- **accept** v 接受
  I accept your apology.
  我接受你的道歉。

Daily Vocabulary 语言学校都会教的实用日常单词
05-06

1 department store 百货公司

shopping mall [ph]	购物中心
plaza ['plɑːzə] [n]	购物广场
outlet ['aʊtlet] [n]	折扣店
community mall [ph]	社区购物中心
neighborhood center [ph]	邻里型购物中心

2 service 服务

information desk [ph]	服务台
customer service [ph]	顾客服务
flyer ['flaɪə] [n]	广告单
parking lot [ph]	停车场
branch [brɑːntʃ] [n]	分店

3 customers 顾客

clerk [klɑːk] [n]	店员	manager ['mænɪdʒə] [n]	经理
attendant [ə'tendənt] [n]	服务员	elevator operator [ph]	电梯服务员
assistant [ə'sɪstənt] [n]	助理		

④ pay 付钱

check [tʃek] [n]		支票
cash [kæʃ] [n]		现金
note [nəʊt] [n]		钞券
coin [kɔɪn] [n]		硬币
card machine [ph]		信用卡刷卡机
credit card [ph]		信用卡
debit card [ph]		现金卡
loyalty card [ph]		积分卡

⑤ casual wear 休闲服饰

jeans [dʒiːnz] [n]		牛仔服饰
swim suit [ph]		泳装
tailor ['teɪlə] [n]		男装
boutique [buːˈtiːk] [n]		女装精品
shoe shop [ph]		鞋店
bedding ['bedɪŋ] [n]		寝具
housewares ['haʊsweəz] [n]		家庭用品

⑥ activity 活动

annual sale [ph]		周年庆
discount ['dɪskaʊnt] [n]		打折
on sale [ph]		拍卖
special offer [ph]		特卖
go window-shopping [ph]		橱窗购物

7 floor 楼层

floor guide [ph]	楼层介绍
elevator ['elɪveɪtə] [n]	电梯
escalator ['eskəleɪtə] [n]	手扶电梯
stairway ['steəweɪ] [n]	楼梯
basement ['beɪsmənt] [n]	地下室

8 merchandise 商品

brand [brænd] [n]	品牌	skin care product [ph]	保养品
fashion ['fæʃn] [n]	时尚	packsack ['pæksæk] [n]	皮制包
consume [kən'sju:m] [n]	消费	jewelry ['dʒu:əlri] [n]	珠宝
shopping ['ʃɒpɪŋ] [n]	购物	purse [pɜːs] [n]	女式手提包
perfume ['pɜːfjuːm] [n]	香水	wallet ['wɒlɪt] [n]	钱包
cosmetic [kɒz'metɪk] [n]	化妆品		

Daily Q&A

[会话一]
Q ▸ Where is the food court?
美食街在哪里？
A ▸ It is in the basement.
在地下室。

[会话二]
Q ▸ Where are the tights?
裤袜在哪里？
A ▸ They are on the 5th floor next to the escalator.
在5楼的手扶电梯旁。

[会话三]
Q ▸ Where can I exchange some free gifts?
我可以在哪里兑换免费商品？
A ▸ Go to the top floor and turn left.
到顶楼左转。

Proverbs & Idioms 地道谚语与惯用语 | 让句子锦上添花

five finger discount 偷窃

Peter got the diamond ring by five finger discount.
彼得偷了一个钻戒。

up for sale 可以购买

The CD will be up for sale in late December. You can not find one in the store now.
在 12 月底就能购买到这片 CD 了。现在你在店里找不到。

garage sale 车库拍卖（在自己家的车库贩卖二手物品）

Jenny has so many things she doesn't need. She plans to have a garage sale to clean out something she has not used them for ages and earn some money.
珍妮有太多不想要的东西了，她计划举办一个车库拍卖，把她多年不用的东西卖掉，顺便换一点现金。

close the sale 成功卖掉某物

Fiona just took out the computer the customer looked for and closed the sale.
费欧娜刚把顾客要找的电脑拿出来，就成功地卖出去了。

elevator music 电梯音乐（在公共场合里所播放的愉悦但单调的音乐）

In some shopping mall you can never get away some elevator music.
在一些购物中心，你永远没有办法摆脱电梯音乐。

gift-wrap something 包装成礼盒

I bought this watch as my boyfriend's birthday gift. Can you please gift-wrap it for me?
我买这只手表给我男朋友做生日礼物。可以请你帮我包装成礼盒吗？

clearance sale 清仓大拍卖

It's the end of the year. A lot of clothing stores are having their clearance sale.
现在是年终。很多服饰店正在清仓大拍卖。

Unit 21 Go to a Night Market 夜市

Daily Conversation 日常对话 | 模拟真实的日常对话

A Let's go to DingDing night market. I miss the taste of stinky tofu and Taiwanese fried chicken.
我们去丁丁夜市吧！我想念臭豆腐和盐酥鸡的味道。

B Me too. When people talk about night markets, the snack food which first comes across my mind is the oyster omelet.
我也是。每次人们提到夜市，在我脑中浮现的小吃是蚵仔煎。

A Oh, my mouth is watering now. Let's set out for the night market.
哦，我开始流口水了。我们现在出发去夜市吧！

B Today is Monday. It is usually not very busy on weekdays.
今天是星期一，工作日里逛夜市的人不会太多。

A I like that. I don't like to walk in the crowds in summer. It makes me sweat all the time.
我喜欢这样。在夏天里，我不喜欢和很多人一起挤。那总是会让我满身大汗。

B I am thirsty. Look at the sign across from the Tempura stand. It says the papaya milk is buy one get one free. It's cheap!
我好渴。看看天妇罗摊对面的那个招牌，上面写说，木瓜牛奶买一送一，真便宜！

Additional Vocabulary & Phrases | 补充单词 & 短语

- **stinky** [a] 臭的
  Your socks are stinky!
  你的袜子真臭！

- **papaya** [n] 木瓜
  My favorite fruit is papaya.
  我最喜欢的水果是木瓜。

- **set out** [ph] 出发
  They set out at six o'clock to the airport.
  他们六点钟出发去机场。

- **sweat** [v] 出汗
  Dan was sweating due to the hot temperature.
  丹因为温度太高而一直出汗。

Daily Sentences 高频用句 | 一分钟学一句，不怕不够用
MP3 05-08

- China is famous for a great **variety** of snack food.
  中国以各式各样的小吃闻名。

- Can you tell me where I can find the **stinky tofu** *1 **stand**?
  你可以告诉我哪里可以找到臭豆腐摊吗？

- It is so crowded here. I am lost.
  这里好挤，我迷路了。

- Can you **recommend** some delicious Guangdong traditional snacks to me?
  你可以推荐我一些好吃的广东传统小吃吗？

- What time do the stands usually come out? What time do they usually finish their business for today?
  这些小摊贩什么时候出摊？他们什么时候会结束当天的营业？

- What do you like to do at a night market?
  你喜欢在夜市做什么？

- Can you show me the meat ball stand shown in my **guide** book at this night market?
  你可以告诉我，这本旅游书上介绍的这个夜市肉丸摊在哪吗？

- Have you ever played **net fish** *2?
  你玩过捞鱼吗？

★ 换个单词说说看 | 用单词丰富句子，让句子更漂亮！

Additional Vocabulary & Phrases | 补充单词 & 短语

- **variety** [n] 多样化、种类
  Sandy has a variety of interests.
  辛蒂有很多种不同的嗜好。

- **stand** [n] 摊子
  This shaved ice stand is very famous.
  这个刨冰摊很有名。

- **recommend** [v] 推荐
  Can you recommend me some books to read?
  你能推荐我一些书吗？

- **guide** [n] 向导、指南
  Katy is an experienced tour guide.
  凯蒂是一位很有经验的导游。

Daily Vocabulary 语言学校都会教的实用日常单词
MP3 05-09

① Taiwanese fried chicken 盐酥鸡

stinky tofu [ph]	臭豆腐
tempura ['tempʊrə] [n]	天妇罗
meat ball [ph]	肉圆
hot dog [ph]	热狗
delicacy ['delɪkəsi] [n]	美味、佳肴

② sausage 香肠

roasted corn on the cob [ph]	烤玉米
chicken claw/feet [ph]	鸡爪
pig's blood rice pudding [ph]	猪血糕
oyster omelet [ph]	蚵仔煎
oyster vermicelli [ph]	蚵仔面

③ Taiwanese sausage with sticky rice 大肠包小肠

| fish ball soup [ph] | 鱼丸汤 | three-cup chicken [ph] | 三杯鸡 |
| hot and sour soup [ph] | 酸辣汤 | salted chicken [ph] | 盐水鸡 |

4 wheel pie 车轮饼

cream [kriːm] [n]	⋯⋯	奶油
red bean [ph]	⋯⋯	红豆
sesame [ˈsesəmi] [n]	⋯⋯	芝麻
taro [ˈtɑːrəʊ] [n]	⋯⋯	芋头
peanut [ˈpiːnʌt] [n]	⋯⋯	花生
dried/pickled radish [ph]	⋯⋯	萝卜干
dried/pickled cabbage [ph]	⋯⋯	高丽菜

5 watermelon juice 西瓜汁

sugar cane juice [ph]	⋯⋯	甘蔗汁
plum juice [ph]	⋯⋯	酸梅汤
pearl milk tea [ph]	⋯⋯	珍珠奶茶
star fruit juice [ph]	⋯⋯	杨桃汤
papaya milk [ph]	⋯⋯	木瓜牛奶
fruit stand [ph]	⋯⋯	水果摊

6 ice 冰

shredded ice [ph]	⋯⋯	刨冰
snowflake ice [ph]	⋯⋯	雪花冰
ice cream [ph]	⋯⋯	冰淇淋
soybean pudding [ph]	⋯⋯	豆花
shaved ice mountain [ph]	⋯⋯	刨冰山

7 vendor 小贩

stand [stænd] [n]		路边摊
decoration [ˌdekəˈreɪʃn] [n]		装饰品
characteristic [ˌkærəktəˈrɪstɪk] [n]		特色
traditional [trəˈdɪʃənl] [a]		传统的
cultural [ˈkʌltʃərəl] [a]		文化的

8 crane games 夹娃娃机

marbles [ˈmɑːblz] [n]	弹珠游戏		**net fish** [ph]	捞鱼
water ballons [ph]	水球		**dolls** [dɒlz] [n]	娃娃
darts [dɑːtz] [n]	飞镖		**mahjong** [n]	麻将

Daily Q&A

〔会话一〕

Q▶ Sir, I would like to have a large papaya milk with less sugar and ice.
先生，我想要一杯大杯木瓜牛奶，少糖少冰。

A▶ No problem.
没问题。

〔会话二〕

Q▶ Would you like some chili sauce on the side of your plate?
你要在盘子旁边放一些辣椒酱吗？

A▶ Sure.
好啊！

〔会话三〕

Q▶ Would you like some shaved ice?
你想要来点刨冰吗？

A▶ No, thanks.
不了，谢谢！

Proverbs & Idioms 地道谚语与惯用语 | 让句子锦上添花

a drug on the market 充斥市场
Right now, small computers are a drug in the market.
现在，迷你电脑充斥整个市场。

like a blind dog in a meat market 失控
The kids played around the museum like blind dogs in a meat market, touching everything they were not supposed to touch.
那些小孩在博物馆里玩到失控，碰了他们不应该碰的所有东西。

a cattle market 声色场所
The nightclub is actually a cattle market. You can always see some sexy bikini girls dance on the stage.
事实上那家夜店是个声色场所，你总是可以看到一些性感的比基尼女郎在舞台上跳舞。

on the market 出售
Kelly put her car on the market last month.
凯莉上个月把她的车卖掉了。

in the market for something 有兴趣购买
I am in the market for a new cell phone. My old one is not working.
我想购买一个新的手机，我的旧手机已经坏了。

price sb. or sth. out of the market 用价格垄断市场淘汰某人或某事
The discount prices posted by the chain store were meant to price us out of the market.
连锁店刊登的优惠价格注定将垄断市场，把我们淘汰出市场。

corner the market on something 让某物独占市场
The company sought to corner the market on their new cellphones.
那公司寻求让他们的新手机独占市场。

crowd together 聚集在一起
Many food stands crowded together to sell delicious food to customers who came to the night market for good food.
很多小吃摊聚集一起贩卖美味的食物给那些来夜市吃美食的客人。

Everyday Sentences 语言学校独家传授的必备好句子

- Can you name some famous snack food in this night market?
  你可以说出这个夜市一些有名的小吃吗？

- My favorite snacks are stinky tofu, oyster omelet, and pearl milk tea.
  我最喜欢的小吃是臭豆腐、蚵仔煎和珍珠奶茶。

- The fruit stand is in the middle next to a shredded ice stand.
  水果摊在夜市中间，刨冰摊的旁边。

- Don't be panic. Just follow the crowds and they will lead you to the next exit.
  不要慌，只要跟着人群走，他们会带你到下一个出口。

- It is usually not easy to get a place to eat some popular snack food like stinky tofu.
  要吃像臭豆腐一样的小吃也很难有位子。

- Look at the Tampura stand over there. You are not possible to eat it on the weekends since it is recently reported to be the most delicious stand in this night market.
  看那边那个天妇罗摊。假日时，你是不可能吃到天妇罗的，因为它最近被报道为这个夜市里最好吃的小吃摊。

- What is the smell coming from? It smells so good.
  那个味道是从哪里来的？很好闻！

- I love roasted corn on a cob.
  我超喜欢烤玉米。

- Do you see the old lady standing over there? She can make the most delicious pig's blood rice pudding in Taibei.
  你看到正站在那边的老妇人了吗？她会做台北最好吃的猪血糕！

MEMO

From AM-PM 从早到晚都用得到的必备好句子

- I want a dress that's shorter.
  我想要买短一点的连衣裙。

- I'm looking for some running shoes.
  我想找慢跑鞋。

- Do you know your shoe size?
  你知道你鞋子的尺寸吗？

- Do you want to cook an egg in a pot?
  你想要把蛋打进锅里煮吗？

- Eating hot pot is really good on cold days.
  冷天吃火锅真是棒极了。

- This hot pot restaurant is all-you-can-eat.
  这家火锅店可以吃到饱。

- Could we eat and watch TV at the same time?
  我们可以边吃饭边看电视吗？

- Don't chew with your mouth open.
  嚼食物时嘴巴不要张开。

- You shouldn't be picky about what you eat.
  你不该挑食。

- The specialty here is Peking duck.
  这里的招牌菜就是北京烤鸭。

- I need some coffee to wake me up.
  我需要一些咖啡来提神。

MEMO

- I prefer iced coffee over hot coffee.
  和热咖啡比起来，我比较想喝冰咖啡。

- Could I have extra cream for my coffee?
  可以帮我在咖啡里多加一些奶油吗？

- The coffee here is freshly brewed.
  这里的咖啡是现煮的。

- Game time! Let's play games.
  游戏时间！我们来玩游戏吧。

- What's the progress on your assignment?
  你工作进度如何？

- Do you have any new updates for me?
  有新进展吗？

- I think I caught a cold.
  我想我感冒了。

- Don't worry about work.
  不要担心工作。

- Could someone turn on the air conditioner?
  谁能把空调打开？

- Put on your socks.
  穿上你的袜子。

- Comb your hair.
  把头发梳一梳。

MEMO

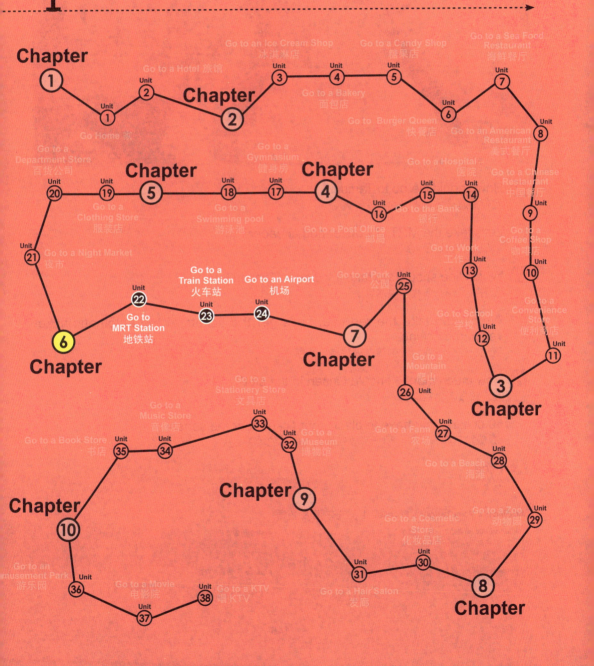

Unit 22 Go to MRT Station 地铁站

Daily Conversation 日常对话 | 模拟真实的日常对话

A How should we go to Tamsui?
我们要怎么去淡水？

B Let's take the MRT. It's faster and cheaper.
我们坐轻轨好了，轻轨又快又便宜。

A Which line should we take if we go to Tamsui?
我们要坐哪一条线到淡水？

B We should take the red line. Let's get the tickets at the **automatic** ticket vending machine.
我们应该坐红线。我们到自动售票机买票吧！

A How much money should I **insert** in the **slot**?
我应该投多少钱进去？

B 50 dollars. You have to **place** your ticket near the sensor.
50 美元。等一下你必须把票放在靠近感应器的地方。

A I see.
我懂了。

Additional Vocabulary & Phrases | 补充单词 & 短语

- **automatic** [a] 自动的、自动装置的
  This dish washer is automatic.
  这个洗碗机是全自动的。

- **insert** [v] 插入、嵌入
  Please insert your card here.
  请将卡片插入这里。

- **slot** [n] 投币孔
  You can insert coin into the slot.
  你可以将硬币投入投币孔。

- **place** [v] 放置、安置
  Please place your cup on the cupboard.
  请将你的杯子放在杯架上。

Daily Sentences 高频用句 | 一分钟学一句，不怕不够用
06-02

- How can I take the MRT?
  我该怎么搭轻轨呢？

- Elvis, put your **cola** *1 away before **entering** the MRT station.
  艾维斯，进轻轨站前先把可乐喝完。

- Watch out! The train is coming. Stand behind the yellow line. It's dangerous.
  小心！火车要来了，你要站在黄线后面。这样很危险！

- Which line should I take to get to **Taipei City Zoo** *2 by MRT?
  哪条轻轨线可以到台北市动物园？

- Please **yield** your seats to the elderly, **pregnant** women and the **handicapped**.
  请让座给老人、孕妇和行动不便者。

- You need to change the train at Taipei Main Station to go to Tamsui.
  你必须在台北车站换乘到淡水。

- Look at the sign over there on the wall. It says "No drinking and eating behind the yellow line." If you do not follow the rules, you will be asked to pay a fine of up to 6,000 dollars.
  看看墙上那张标语。标语上写着"黄线内禁止饮食"。如果你不遵守规定，将会被罚款 6 000 美元。

★ 换个单词说说看 | 用单词丰富句子，让句子更漂亮！

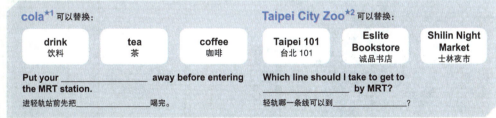

Additional Vocabulary & Phrases | 补充单词 & 短语

- **enter** [v] 进入
  She just entered the building.
  她刚刚才进入大楼里。

- **yield** [v] 让分
  Please yield your seat to those in need.
  请让位给需要的乘客。

- **pregnant** [a] 怀孕的
  Mia is pregnant.
  米雅怀孕了。

- **handicapped** [a] 有生理残缺的
  The handicapped doesn't mean useless.
  有生理残缺的人不代表没有用。

Daily Vocabulary 语言学校都会教的实用日常单词

1 Mass Rapid Transit (MRT) 轻轨

subway ['sʌbweɪ] [n]		地铁
metro ['metrəʊ] [n]		捷运
The Underground [ph]		英国地铁
The Tube [ph]		英国地铁
public transportation [ph]		大众交通工具

2 station 车站

terminal station [ph]	终点站
transfer station [ph]	转乘站
regular station [ph]	一般车站
automatic platform gate [ph]	安全闸门
exit ['eksɪt] [n]	出口

3 ticket 票、券、车票、入场券

automatic ticket vending machine [ph]	自动售票机	**sensor** ['sensə] [n]		感应器
scan the ticket [ph]	感应票卡	**single-journey ticket** [ph]		单程票
easy card [ph]	储值卡	**unregistered** [ˌʌn'redʒɪstəd] [a]		没记录到
top up [ph]	储值			

4 platform 月台

platform gap [ph]	————	月台与列车的间隙
elevator ['elɪveɪtə] [n]	————	电梯
escalator ['eskəleɪtə] [n]	————	手扶电梯
handrail ['hændreɪl] [n]	————	把手
prohibit [prə'hɪbɪt] [v]	————	禁止
food and drink [ph]	————	饮食

5 car 车厢

priority seat [ph]	————	爱心座椅
wheelchair accessible [ph]	————	无障碍空间
yield [ji:ld] [v]	————	礼让
emergency fire extinguisher [ph]	————	紧急灭火器
seat [si:t] [n]	————	座位
grip [grɪp] [v]	————	紧握

6 tourist 旅游者、观光者

route map [ph]	————	路线图
timetable ['taɪmteɪbl] [n]	————	时刻表
ticket fare [ph]	————	车票费
bulletin board [ph]	————	布告栏
easy mall [ph]	————	地下商城

7 passenger service 乘客服务

information counter [ph]	服务台
station staff [ph]	站务人员
weekday ['wi:kdeɪ] [n]	平日、工作日
peak hour [ph]	高峰时刻
off-peak hour [ph]	非高峰时刻
holiday ['hɒlədeɪ] [n]	假日

8 passenger 乘客

elder ['eldə] [n]	老人	children ['tʃɪldrən] [n]	儿童
senior citizen [ph]	年长者	adult ['ædʌlt] [n]	成人
pregnant woman [ph]	孕妇	restroom for the handicapped [ph]	无障碍厕所
indigenous people [ph]	低收入者		

Daily Q&A

〔会话一〕

Q▶ Excuse me. Which line should I take to get to Taipei Zoo by MRT?
请问一下，轻轨哪一条线可以到动物园？

A▶ You should take the brown line.
你要搭棕线。

〔会话二〕

Q▶ How much is the ticket from Taipei Train Station to Tamsui?
从台北火车站到淡水票价多少？

A▶ It's 50 dollars.
50 美元。

〔会话三〕

Q▶ Excuse me. Where can I buy the ticket?
不好意思，我在哪里可以买到票？

A▶ You can buy it at the automatic ticket vending machine.
你可以在自动售票机买票。

Proverbs & Idioms 地道谚语与惯用语 | 让句子锦上添花

hot ticket 热门的人事
Singers who can dance now are a hot ticket right now.
现在会跳舞的歌手很热门。

get one's ticket punched 死亡
Poor Greg! He got his ticket punched while he was waiting for a bus.
可怜的桂格！他等公车的时候去世了。

just a ticket 完美的事物
A bowl of hot soup is just a ticket in a freezing day.
在寒冷的日子里来一碗热汤是件完美的事。

round-trip ticket 往返票
A round-trip ticket is usually cheaper than a one-way ticket. If you want to go to Tainan by High Speed Railway, buy a round-trip ticket. You may have some discount.
往返票通常比单程票便宜。如果你要搭高铁去台南，买张往返票吧！你可以有一些折扣。

big ticket 昂贵的物品
Not many people can afford buying big ticket items when the economy is bad.
不是所有人在经济不景气时都买得起昂贵的物品。

a one-way ticket to something 无法避免的坏事
As far as I am concerned, being addicted to the drugs is a one-way ticket to misery and poor health.
对我来说有毒瘾是一件无法避免的坏事，不但会带来不幸，也有损健康。

go off the rails 行为不当
That famous singer went off the rails again last weekend. He yelled at his fans and tried to attack them for no reason.
那位著名的歌手上周末行为不当。他无理地对他的粉丝大吼并试图攻击他们。

off the beaten track 鲜有人出没的地方
That restaurant is difficult to find. It is really off the beaten track.
那家餐厅很难被找到。它一定在鲜有人出没的地方。

Unit 23 Go to a Train Station 火车站

Daily Conversation 日常对话 | 模拟真实的日常对话

06-04

B Wow. There are so many passengers on this train.
哇！火车上好多乘客！

A There are. This is maybe because we have a long weekend. Many people want to take a trip to Hsinchu.
是啊！这是因为我们这周末有长假，很多人想去新竹玩。

B Well, maybe. Can you find our seats?
嗯，也许吧。你找得到我们的位子吗？

A Let me check our tickets… It says Row 12 A and B.
让我看看我们的车票……上面写着 12 排 A 和 B。

B Look! Our seats are over there. 12 A is the window seat and 12 B is the aisle seat.
你看，我们的座位在那里。12A 是靠窗的座位，12B 是靠走道的座位。

A Great! I like the window seat. It is more comfortable.
太好了！我喜欢靠窗的位子，比较舒服。

Additional Vocabulary & Phrases | 补充单词 & 短语

- **row** n 列、排
  Which row do you sit?
  你坐哪一排？

- **window** n 窗户
  Can you open the window?
  可以请你打开窗户吗？

- **aisle** n 通道、走道
  Please do not block the aisle.
  请不要阻挡通道。

- **comfortable** a 舒服的
  It's so comfortable sitting on the sofa.
  坐在沙发上真的很舒服。

Daily Sentences 高频用句 | 一分钟学一句，不怕不够用

- Excuse me. We would like a one-way ticket to Taichung*1.
  不好意思，我们要一张到台中的单程车票。

- Would you be nice enough to find me a seat near the window? I am afraid of getting car sick.
  你可不可以帮我安排一个靠窗的位子？我怕晕车。

- Look! There is a long line. Every one is lining up to buy tickets.
  看！好长的队伍，每个人都排队买票。

- We should have bought the tickets online.
  我应该网上购票的。

- Ma'am, I would like a round-trip ticket to Tainan.
  女士，我要一张到台南的往返票。

- Look at the timetable. The train to Taoyuan departs at 6:20 and arrives at 6:45.
  看看时刻表，到桃园的火车 6:20 离开，6:45 到达。

- Can I have a timetable for the High Speed Rail?
  可以给我一张高铁的车次表吗？

- Where is the ticket booth*2?
  售票亭在哪里？

- Do you have your ticket with you? The train ticket puncher will punch the tickets before we get on the train.
  你带车票了吗？检票员会在我们上火车时检票。

★ 换个单词说说看 | 用单词丰富句子，让句子更漂亮！

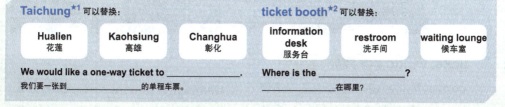

Daily Vocabulary 语言学校都会教的超用日常单词

1 train 列车、火车

rail [reɪl] n	轨道
railroad ['reɪlrəʊd] n	铁路
railway ['reɪlweɪ] n	铁路系统
track [træk] n	铁轨
carriage ['kærɪdʒ] n	车厢

2 bullet train 子弹列车

express train ph	特快列车
high speed rail ph	高铁列车
ordinary train ph	普通列车
local express ph	普快列车
limited express ph	特快列车

3 ticket window 售票处

convenience [kən'viːniəns] n	方便
information desk ph	服务台
a long line ph	排长队
train ticket puncher ph	火车检票员
waiting lounge ph	候车室

④ timetable 时刻表

passenger ['pæsɪndʒə] [n]	……	乘客
tourist ['tʊərɪst] [n]	……	旅游者
luggage ['lʌgɪdʒ] [n]	……	行李
train announcer [ph]	……	火车播音员
ticket gate [ph]	……	检票口

⑤ conductor 列车长

train master compartment [ph]	……	列车长室
fare adjustment [ph]	……	补票
one way trip [ph]	……	单程
round trip [ph]	……	往返
train staff [ph]	……	火车服务员

⑥ seat number 座位号码

window seat [ph]	……	靠窗的座位
aisle seat [ph]	……	靠走道的座位
wheelchair accessible car [ph]	……	无障碍车厢
row [rəʊ] [n]	……	一列座位、一排座位
smoking car [ph]	……	吸烟车厢
unreserved seat [ph]	……	自由座
reserved seat [ph]	……	对号座

7 compartment 火车包厢

food trolley [ph] .... 餐车
sales trolley [ph] .... 商品推车
first class [ph] .... 头等舱
stateroom ['steɪtruːm] [n] .... 火车卧铺
kitchenette [ˌkɪtʃɪ'net] [n] .... 茶水间

8 platform 月台

locomotive [ˌləʊkə'məʊtɪv] [n] .... 火车头
station master ['steɪʃən 'mɑːstə] .... 火车站长
station attendant [ph] .... 站务员
direction [də'rekʃn] [n] .... 方向
main line [ph] .... 主干线

time required [ph] .... 行车时间
destination [ˌdestɪ'neɪʃn] [n] .... 终点
terminal ['tɜːmɪnl] [n] .... 终点站
last train [ph] .... 末班车
first train [ph] .... 首班车

Daily Q&A

〔会话一〕
Q▶ Excuse me! When will the train to Tainan depart?
不好意思！到台南的车几点离开？
A▶ It'll leave for Tainan at 14:30.
它将于 14:30 前往台南。

〔会话二〕
Q▶ How much does the High Speed Rail ticket to Taoyun cost?
到桃园的高铁车票多少钱？
A▶ It costs 200 dollars.
约 200 美元。

〔会话三〕
Q▶ Where is Platform 5?
第五站台在哪里？
A▶ It's on the second floor. Walk up the stairs and turn right. It's on your right.
在二楼。走上楼梯右转，就在你右手边。

Proverbs & Idioms　**地道谚语与惯用语｜让句子锦上添花**

the gravy train　过奢华的生活
Many people think they can get on the gravy train by winning the lottery.
很多人以为他们可以靠中彩票来过上奢华的生活。

on the hot seat　众人批评的焦点
Kevin said something wrong in front of the ladies. He is on the hot seat now.
凯文在女士们面前说错了话，他现在是众人批评的焦点。

on the edge of one's seat　跟随表演情绪起伏
The play was so good. We sat on the edge of our seats of the whole play.
那部剧真好看。我们的情绪跟随着整个剧情而起伏。

in the driver's seat　掌控主导某事
Tina can't wait to get into the driver's seat to do what she can turn things around.
蒂娜等不及掌控她可以扭转乾坤的事。

in the catbird seat　在主导控制的位子、处于有利地位
I have all the power in deciding things. I am in the catbird seat.
我有决定的权力。我在主导控制的位子。

a train of thought　一连串的思维
Don't interrupt my train of thought. I need to think this through with full concentration.
不要打断我的思绪。我需要全神贯注地思考这件事。

depart for …(place)　前往……（地点）
When do we depart for New York?
我们什么时候前往纽约？

set in train　开始某事
His protest in front of the presidential hall set in train the event which finally led to revolution.
他在总统府前的抗议最终导致了一场革命。

Unit 24 Go to an Airport 机场

Daily Conversation 日常对话 | 模拟真实的日常对话

A The seats are pretty big although we are in the economy class section.
虽然我们是在经济舱，座位还是挺大的。

B Yup. The flight attendants are pretty and charming. That is why I love taking Dongfang Airline so much.
是呀！空姐都很漂亮、迷人。这就是为什么我这么喜欢搭乘东方航空。

A Indeed. Every one of us has a personal TV. We can watch the programs we like without sharing with other people.
的确。每个人都有一台电视。我们可以看自己喜欢的节目，而不用和别人共用电视。

B We are lucky. We are sitting near the lavatory right next to the emergency exit.
我们很幸运。我们就坐在靠近紧急逃生口的厕所旁边。

A Yeah. I want a blanket and a pillow. Where are the earphones?
是呀！我想要一块毛毯和一个枕头。耳机在哪里呢？

B They are in the seat pocket in front of you.
就在你座位前方的袋子中。

Additional Vocabulary & Phrases | 补充单词 & 短语

- **charming** [a] 迷人的
  Sandy is a charming girl.
  桑迪是一位迷人的女孩。

- **lucky** [a] 幸运的
  Violet was lucky that she won the lottery.
  薇莉特很幸运赢得彩票。

- **emergency** [a] 紧急的
  This was an emergency case.
  这是一个紧急的案件。

- **pillow** [n] 枕头
  I need to buy a new pillow.
  我需要买一个新枕头。

Daily Sentences 高频用句 | 一分钟学一句，不怕不够用
MP3 06-08

- Excuse me ma'am. I would like my luggage checked all the way to Japan. I will need to transfer at L.A. I don't want to claim my luggage and check in again. That is a tiring job.
  小姐，不好意思，我想把行李直接运送到日本。我必须在洛杉矶转机，我不想把行李拿出又入关一次，那是一件很累人的事。

- Here are your luggage claim tags*¹.
  这是你行李的条码。

- Here is your boarding pass. Your flight is at Gate 12. Please arrive at the gate 30 minutes before take off.
  这是你的登机卡。你的飞机在 12 号登机口。请于飞机起飞前 30 分钟到达登机门。

- We would like to look for the information desk and ask if there is a currency exchange desk in the airport.
  我想找询问台，咨询机场里有没有可以兑换货币的地方。

- Look at the catalogue for the online duty free shop. The LB bags come in 12 different colors. I definitely want one.
  看一看网上免税商店的目录。LB 的袋子有 12 种不同的颜色，我当然要一个。

- We will need to check in 3 hours ahead of the departure time.
  我会在起飞前 3 小时入关。

- Excuse me. I would like to get my tax refund at the airport. Where is the refund counter?
  不好意思，我想在机场退税。退税柜台在哪里？

- Where can I find the carts at the airport? I need one to carry all my luggage.
  我可以在机场的什么地方找到推车？我需要一台来推我的行李。

★ 换个单词说说看 | 用单词丰富句子，让句子更漂亮！

luggage claim tags*¹ 可以替换：

| boarding pass 登机卡 | passport 护照 | Here are your _____. 这是你的_____。 |

Additional Vocabulary & Phrases | 补充单词 & 短语

- **claim** [v] 要求、索取
  Where can I claim my baggage?
  我能到哪里拿我的行李呢？

- **take off** [ph] 起飞
  The plane will take off in 30 minutes.
  飞机将在 30 分钟后起飞。

- **refund** [v][n] 退还、退款
  I need to get my refund.
  我需要拿到我的退款。

- **cart** [n] 推车
  Where are the carts?
  推车在哪呢？

161

Daily Vocabulary 语言学校都会教的实用日常单词
06-09

1 terminal 机场航厦

domestic terminal [ph]	国内航站楼
departure lobby [ph]	出境大厅
information desk [ph]	询问柜台
shuttle bus [ph]	机场巴士
currency exchange [ph]	外币兑换处
insurance counter [ph]	保险柜台

2 check-in counter 登机报到柜台

passenger ['pæsɪndʒə] [n]	旅客
customer service [ph]	航空柜台人员
ground staff [ph]	地勤人员
airline service counter [ph]	航空公司服务柜台
luggage tag [ph]	行李吊牌
luggage scale [ph]	行李磅秤

3 baggage 行李

baggage claim [ph]	提领行李	skycap ['skaɪkæp] [n]	机场行李搬运员
baggage delivery [ph]	行李托运	luggage carousel [ph]	行李输送台
carry-on bag [ph]	随身行李		
luggage cart [ph]	行李推车		

4 customs 海关

x-ray machine [ph] —— X 光检测机
passport ['pɑːspɔːt] [n] —— 护照
metal detector [ph] —— 金属探测器
security check [ph] —— 安全检查
immigration [ˌɪmɪˈɡreɪʃn] [n] —— 出入境
duty-free shop [ph] —— 免税商店

5 boarding 登机

boarding gate [ph] —— 登机门
boarding pass [ph] —— 登机卡
delay [dɪˈleɪ] [n] —— 误点
on time [ph] —— 准时
departure [n] —— 出境
greeting area [ph] —— 到站等候区

6 airplane 飞机

runway [ˈrʌnweɪ] [n] —— 跑道
control tower [ph] —— 塔台
air bridge [ph] —— 空桥
apron [ˈeɪprən] [n] —— 停机坪
remote parking bay [ph] —— 接驳机坪

7 cabin crew 空服人员

flight attendant [ph]	空乘人员
captain ['kæptɪn] [n]	机长
copilot ['koʊˌpaɪlət] [n]	副机长
first class [ph]	头等舱
business class [ph]	商务舱
economy class [ph]	经济舱

8 in-flight meal 飞机餐

tray [treɪ] [n]	机上餐桌
trolley ['trɒli] [n]	餐车
call button [ph]	服务铃
in-flight sale [ph]	机上免税品出售
window blinds [ph]	遮阳板
seat belt [ph]	安全带

window seat [ph]	靠窗的座位
aisle seat [ph]	靠走道的座位
overhead compartment [ph]	舱顶置物柜
lavatory ['lævətri] [n]	盥洗室
emergency exit [ph]	紧急出口

Daily Q&A

〔会话一〕

Q▶ Do you know where I can claim the luggage?
你知道在哪里取回我们的行李吗？

A▶ It's on the second floor.
在二楼。

〔会话二〕

Q▶ I would like to find the VIP Lounge.
我想知道贵宾室在哪里。

A▶ Just follow the red sign. You can find it.
只要跟着红标走，你就会找到那个地方。

〔会话三〕

Q▶ Where is the duty free shop?
免税商店在哪里？

A▶ It's at Terminal 2.
在第二航站楼。

Proverbs & Idioms 地道谚语与惯用语 | 让句子锦上添花

a flight of fantasy 虚华不实的梦想

Do you mean you want to go cycling across the U.S.A.? Well, I think that is another flight of fantasy.
你是说想骑自行车横越美国？嗯，我想那是一个虚华不实的梦想。

in flight 飞机航程中

A passenger had a heart attack in flight. The plane had to have an emergency landing in Mongolia.
有一个乘客在飞机上突发心脏病，飞机必须紧急迫降蒙古国。

in full flight 快速逃跑

The bank robber was in full flight before the bank manager called the police.
劫匪在银行经理叫警察之前快速逃跑了。

the top flight 排名第一

Yankee is always the top flight among all the baseball teams in every season.
洋基队一直以来在每一赛季的所有棒球队中排名第一。

depart from one place 从（某处）离开

We will depart from Taipei on time. In a few hours, we will arrive in L.A.
我们将从台北准时离开。几小时之后我们就会到达洛杉矶。

It's better to travel hopefully than to arrive. 享受事情的过程

You should concentrate on enjoying your school life instead of getting a diploma or a degree. It's better to travel hopefully than to arrive.
你应该专注于享受你的学生生活，而不是获得证书或文凭。要享受事情的过程。

on schedule 按照行程计划表走

The trains run pretty much on schedule except for the bad weather condition.
这些火车大多数按照行程计划表行驶，除非天气不佳。

behind schedule 行程计划延迟

The project is behind schedule because some workers are sick and have to take some days off.
这项计划行程延迟，因为一些工人生病必须放几天假。

Everyday Sentences 语言学校独家传授的必备好句子

- The customs need some time to examine every passenger in order to secure the flight safety.
  海关人员需要时间检查每位乘客以确保飞行安全。

- You can find the duty-free shop next to the luggage claim section. But, I think you need some coins.
  你可以在行李取回处的旁边找到免税店。不过,我想你需要一些零钱。

- We would like to welcome you to take Dongfang Airline. Before the airplane takes off, please pay attention to a video clip about the flight security.
  欢迎搭乘东方航空,在飞机起飞前,请注意看一段飞机安全事项的影片。

- Oh, we need to fasten our seat belt, turn off the mobile phone, put up you tray and put the seat in the upright position.
  喔,我们要系紧安全带、关掉手机、把餐盘收起,并把椅背拉直。

- I am almost ready to take a good rest on the plane.
  我已经完全准备好在飞机上好好休息了。

- The airplane is taking off in 5 minutes! We can do whatever we like after taking off.
  飞机再过 5 分钟就起飞了!我们可以在起飞后做任何想做的事。

- I think you need to prepare your passport when you shop at the duty-free shop.
  你在免税店购物应该需要你的护照。

- Where is the boarding gate?
  登机门在哪?

- What time does the plane take off?
  飞机几点起飞?

- Our destination is Thailand.
  我们的目的地是泰国。

MEMO

From AM-PM 从早到晚都用得到的必备好句子

- I'll grab a bite to eat on the way to work.
  我会拿一点在上班路上吃。

- We're out of coffee. How about some milk instead?
  我们没有咖啡了,喝牛奶怎么样?

- Wake up, sleepy head!
  起床了,贪睡虫!

- Oh no! I overslept!
  喔,不!我睡过头了!

- I can't decide what to wear today.
  我无法决定今天要穿什么。

- I had a weird dream last night.
  我昨晚做了个奇怪的梦。

- Let me wash my face first.
  让我先洗脸。

- Drinking a glass of warm milk might help you sleep.
  喝一杯温牛奶也许对你的睡眠有帮助。

- I might watch TV since I can't sleep.
  我既然睡不着,不如看一下电视吧。

- Could you talk to me on the phone until I fall asleep?
  你能跟我打电话聊到我睡着吗?

- You look like you need some sleep.
  你看起来需要好好睡一下。

MEMO

- Why are you still awake?
  你怎么还醒着？

- It's late! Go to bed!
  很晚了！去睡觉！

- Could you turn off the lights, please?
  请把灯关掉，好吗？

- I need to take my contact lenses off before I go to sleep.
  我睡觉前得先摘掉隐形眼镜。

- I want to finish reading my book before bedtime.
  我想在睡前把书看完。

- Could you please turn down the radio so I can study?
  能请你把收音机声音关小吗？这样我才能学习。

- I like to play with my toys.
  我想玩我的玩具。

- Have you ever tried grilled squid?
  你吃过烤鱿鱼吗？

- This night market is famous for snake soup.
  这个夜市以蛇汤闻名。

- We can have some shaved ice here.
  我们可以在这里吃刨冰。

- There are many night markets around Taipei city.
  台北附近有很多夜市。

MEMO

Chapter 7
Close to Nature
享受大自然

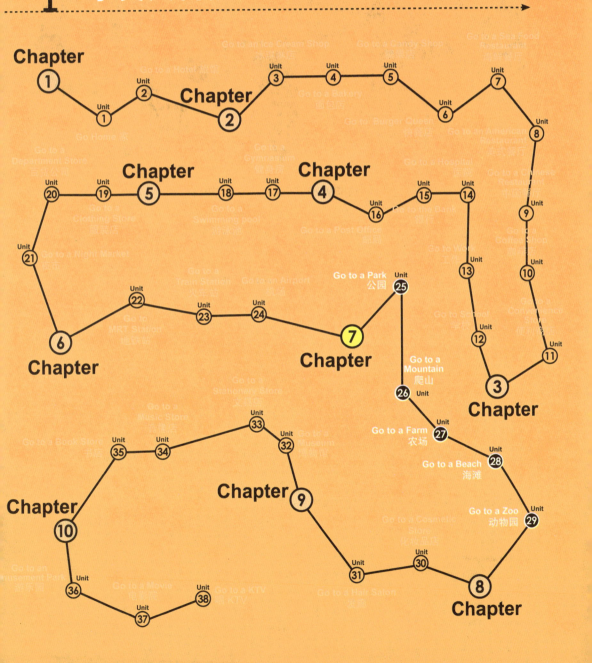

Unit 25 Go to a Park 公园

Daily Conversation 日常对话 | 模拟真实的日常对话

A It's a beautiful day! Let's play on those rides in the park.
天气真好！我们去公园玩那些游乐设施。

B Sounds like a good idea. I love to play on the jungle gym.
听起来不错。我很喜欢玩攀登架。

A Me too. I love to play on the swing as well. The swing is my favorite.
我也是。我还想想玩荡秋千。荡秋千是我的最爱。

B That's great. Then we won't fight about taking the same ride.
那太好了。那么我们就不会抢同一个游乐设施玩了。

A Look at the flowers over there. What are they?
看看那边那些花。那些是什么花呢？

B They are morning glories. They are cute, aren't they?
它们是牵牛花。它们很可爱，不是吗？

A They are. We can find many kinds of flowers and insects in the park.
是啊！我们可以在公园里找到不同种类的花和昆虫。

Additional Vocabulary & Phrases | 补充单词 & 短语

- **jungle** n 丛林
  There are many animals in the jungle.
  在丛林里有很多动物。

- **as well** ph 也
  I am going home and my sister is going as well.
  我要回家，我妹妹也是。

- **fight** v 打架、争吵
  My girlfriend and I have never fought.
  我女友和我从未吵过架。

Daily Sentences 高频用句 | 一分钟学一句,不怕不够用

07-02

- There are so many **flies and mosquitoes** *¹ in the park.
  公园里有很多苍蝇和蚊子。

- You can **apply** some **mosquito spray** before you go there.
  你可以在去那儿之前抹一些防蚊液。

- What is the name of the insect?
  这昆虫叫什么名字?

- Didn't you see the sign? It says "**Keep off** the grass".
  你看到这个标语了吗?上面写着"请勿践踏草坪"。

- Where is the restroom?
  厕所在哪里?

- I am tired. Let's sit on the bench by the pond.
  我很累了。我们在池塘边找一张板凳坐下吧。

- I am hungry. Can we find something to eat?
  我好饿。我们可以找些东西吃吗?

- Can we walk the dog in the park?
  我们可以在公园遛狗吗?

- This insect is a **beetle** *².
  这种昆虫是金龟子。

★ 换个单词说说看 | 用单词丰富句子,让句子更漂亮!

flies and mosquitoes *¹ 可以替换:

| bees 蜜蜂 | butterfly 蝴蝶 | dragonfly 蜻蜓 |

There are so many _____ in the park.
公园里有很多_____。

beetle *² 可以替换:

| locust 蝗虫 | bumblebee 大黄蜂 | silkworm 蚕 |

This insect is _____.
这种昆虫是_____。

Additional Vocabulary & Phrases | 补充单词 & 短语

- **apply** v 申请
  I want to apply for the graduate school in America.
  我想要申请美国的研究所。

- **mosquito** n 蚊子
  There's a mosquito on your arm!
  你的手臂上有一只蚊子!

- **spray** v 喷、洒
  You can spray some water on the plant.
  你可以在植物上喷些水。

- **keep off** ph 远离
  Please keep off that topic.
  请避开那个主题。

Daily Vocabulary 语言学校都会教的实用日常单词

07-03

1 botanical garden 植物园

fern [fɜːn] [n]		蕨类
morning glory [ph]		牵牛花
clover [ˈkləʊvə] [n]		苜蓿
dandelion [ˈdændɪlaɪən] [n]		蒲公英
alfalfa [ælˈfælfə] [n]		紫花苜蓿

2 grass 草

lawn [lɔːn] [n]	草坪
oak [əʊk] [n]	橡树
maple tree [ph]	枫树
bamboo [ˌbæmˈbuː] [n]	竹子
banyan [ˈbænjən] [n]	榕树
bush [bʊʃ] [n]	灌木
petunia [pəˈtjuːniə] [n]	矮牵牛花

3 pavilion 公园中的亭子

shade [ʃeɪd] [n]	树荫处	**wooden** [ˈwʊdn] [a]	木制的
observatory [əbˈzɜːvətri] [n]	瞭望台	**tile** [taɪl] [n]	瓷砖

4 pond 池塘

lake [leɪk] [n]	湖	
wood [wʊd] [n]	树林	
swan [swɒn] [n]	天鹅	
mandarin ducks [ph]	鸳鸯	
mallard duck [ph]	绿头鸭	
feed [fi:d] [v]	喂食	
pigeon ['pɪdʒɪn] [n]	鸽子	

5 bench 长椅

- **path** [pɑ:θ] [n] —— 小路
- **trash can** [ph] —— 垃圾桶
- **fallen leaf** [ph] —— 落叶
- **streetlamp** [stri:t læmp] [n] —— 路灯
- **fence** [fens] [n] —— 栅栏

6 insect 昆虫

- **bee** [bi:] [n] —— 蜜蜂
- **beetle** ['bi:tl] [n] —— 金龟子
- **ant** [ænt] [n] —— 蚂蚁
- **ladybug** ['leɪdibɜ:d] [n] —— 瓢虫
- **mosquito** [mə'ski:təʊ] [n] —— 蚊子
- **fly** [flaɪ] [n] —— 苍蝇

7 walk the dog 遛狗

- **leash** [liːʃ] [n] （拴狗的）皮带、绳
- **Labrador Retriever** [ph] 拉布拉多
- **husky** ['hʌski] [n] 哈士奇
- **Golden Retriever** [ph] 黄金猎犬
- **shiba inu** [ph] 柴犬
- **chihuahua** [n] 吉娃娃

8 playground 游乐场

- **ride** [raɪd] [n] 游乐器材
- **slide** [slaɪd] [n] 滑梯
- **swing** [swing] [n] 秋千
- **seesaw** ['siː sɔː] [n] 跷跷板
- **bars** [baːz] [n] 单杠
- **jungle gym** [ph] 攀爬架
- **sports equipment** [ph] 运动器材
- **toddler** ['tɒdlə] [n] 学步的小孩
- **cycling** ['saɪklɪŋ] [n] 自行车运动
- **roller-blades** ['rəʊlə bleɪdz] [n] 直排轮溜冰鞋

Daily Q&A

〔会话一〕
Q▶ Let's go to the park, shall we?
我们去公园好不好？

A▶ That sounds a good idea.
听起来不错。

〔会话二〕
Q▶ What do you like to play on in the park?
你要在公园玩什么？

A▶ I like to play on the seesaw. It's fun.
我想玩跷跷板，很好玩。

〔会话三〕
Q▶ What is the name of the flower?
这朵花叫什么名字？

A▶ It's morning glory.
这是牵牛花。

Proverbs & Idioms 地道谚语与惯用语 | 让句子锦上添花

a big frog in a small pond 大材小用
Tom is a big frog in a small pond. You need to force him to do something more challenging.
汤姆真的是大材小用了。你要强迫他做一些有挑战性的事情。

squirrel something away 偷藏东西
My father sometimes squirrels some money away before he gives his salary to my mom.
我爸爸有时会在把薪水交给我妈妈之前偷藏私房钱。

a stool pigeon 线人
The policeman got a stool pigeon. That is why he can always get the first-hand news.
那位警察有个线人。这就是为什么他总有第一手消息的原因。

be somebody's pigeon 负责人
Accounting is not my pigeon. You should find Jack.
会计不是我负责的。你要找杰克。

put the cat among the pigeons 闹得鸡飞狗跳
If you tell them this shocking news, I believe that will put the cat among the pigeons.
如果你告诉他们这则惊人的新闻，我相信会闹得鸡飞狗跳。

a walk in the park 轻松有趣的事
Finishing that job is really like a walk in the park. There shouldn't be any problem to him.
完成那项工作是件轻松愉快的事。这对他而言应该没有问题。

a ballpark figure 几近确切的数目
We don't know the actual cost, but a ballpark figure would be about five thousand dollars.
我不知道实际的数目，但是确切的数目应是接近 5 000 美元。

Unit 26 Go to a Mountain 爬山

Daily Conversation 日常对话 | 模拟真实的日常对话

A It's wonderful to be in the mountains after a hustle bustle week.
在忙碌的一周过后跑到山里面是件美好的事。

B Indeed. I love the smell of the grass and trees. They certainly refresh my mind.
没错。我爱极了草和树的味道。它们无疑可以洗净我的心灵。

A Can we stop here for a while? My backpack is very heavy.
我们可以在这里停一下吗？我的背包很重。

B Sure. Did you hear anything? Look! An eagle is hovering in the sky.
当然。你听到声音了吗？看！有一只老鹰在天空中盘旋。

A Let me see. It's not an eagle. I think it's a vulture.
让我瞧瞧。那不是老鹰。我想那是一只秃鹰。

B Yes. Will it hurt us?
对，它会伤害我们吗？

A I don't think so. Let's walk by the stream. I am sure we can find the waterfall on the map.
我不这么认为。我们沿着小溪走。我确定我们一定可以找到地图上的瀑布。

Additional Vocabulary & Phrases | 补充单词 & 短语

- **refresh** [v] 消除……疲劳、重新提起精神
  This energy drink will help you refresh.
  这个能量饮料能帮助你重新提起精神。

- **hover** [v] 盘旋
  The eagle was hovering above us.
  老鹰在我们上空盘旋。

- **vulture** [n] 秃鹰
  I have never seen a vulture.
  我从未见过秃鹰。

- **waterfall** [n] 瀑布
  There's a small waterfall over there.
  那边有一个小瀑布。

Daily Sentences 高频用句 | 一分钟学一句，不怕不够用

07-05

- Where can I find the lake?
  我可以在哪里找到湖？

- You can walk along this path. It goes to a big lake in the mountains.
  你可以沿着这条小路走，这条路会通往一个山里的大湖。

- What is the name of this tree?
  这棵树是什么树？

- This is a **Maple tree** *1.
  这是枫树。

- This road is very **steep**.
  这条路很陡。

- I think we need a **cane**.
  我想我们需要一根拐杖。

- There is a **cable** car to go from one peak to the other. We can take it if we do not want to climb mountains.
  有缆车可从一座山峰通到另一座山峰。如果不想爬山的话，我们可以乘缆车。

- Listen! It is a **humming bird** *2. I can barely see its wings.
  你听！那是只蜂鸟，我几乎看不到它的翅膀。

- It's tiring to **climb** high mountains.
  爬高山很累人的。

★ 换个单词说说看 | 用单词丰富句子，让句子更漂亮！

Additional Vocabulary & Phrases | 补充单词 & 短语

- **steep** a 陡峭的
  This is a steep hill.
  这是一个陡峭的山丘。

- **cane** n 拐杖
  She needed a cane.
  她需要一个拐杖。

- **cable** n 电缆、钢索
  They are fixing the cable.
  他们在修理电缆。

- **climb** v 爬
  Please don't climb up on the table.
  请勿爬到桌子上。

Daily Vocabulary 语言学校都会教的实用日常单词
07-06

1 backpack 登山、远足用的背包

bottle ['bɒtl] [n]	大水罐、水壶
provisions [prə'vɪʒn] [n]	预备的口粮
mountaineering boots [ph]	登山鞋
cane [keɪn] [n]	手杖
compass ['kʌmpəs] [n]	指南针
first-aid kit [ph]	急救包

2 mountain 山（脉）

hill [hɪl] [n] .... 丘陵
mountainside ['maʊntənsaɪd] [n] ...... 山坡、山腰
grassland ['grɑːslænd] [n] .... 草原
forest ['fɒrɪst] [n] .... 森林
path [pɑːθ] [n] .... 小路
stream [striːm] [n] .... 小溪
lake [leɪk] [n] .... 湖
valley ['væli] [n] .... 山谷
waterfall ['wɔːtəfɔːl] [n] .... 瀑布

3 mountain climbing 登山

map [mæp] [n]	地图	cable car [ph]	缆车
guide [gaɪd] [n]	向导	hiking ['haɪkɪŋ] [n]	爬山、健行
peak [piːk] [n]	山顶		

4 forest 森林

pine [paɪn] n	....	松树
cedar ['siːdə] n	....	杉木
birch [bɜːtʃ] n	....	桦树
cypress ['saɪprəs] n	....	桧树
oak [əʊk] n	....	橡树
willow ['wɪləʊ] n	....	柳树

5 bird 鸟、禽

woodpecker ['wʊdpekə] n	....	啄木鸟
hummingbird ['hʌmɪŋbɜːd] n	....	蜂鸟
swallow ['swɒləʊ] n	....	燕子
vulture ['vʌltʃə] n	....	秃鹰
eagle ['iːgl] n	....	鹰

6 wild animals 野生动物

squirrel ['skwɪrəl] n	....	松鼠
black bear ph	....	黑熊
brown bear ph	....	棕熊
raccoon [rəˈkuːn] n	....	浣熊
andean mountain cat ph	....	山猫
chital ['tʃiːtəl] n	....	斑鹿

7 sunset 日落

sunrise ['sʌnraɪz] [n] .... 日出
haze [heɪz] [n] .... 薄雾
mist [mɪst] [n] .... 山岚
fog [fɒg] [n] .... 雾
sea of clouds [ph] .... 云海

8 monkey 猴子

ape [eɪp] [n] .... 大猩猩
mandrill ['mændrɪl] [n] .... 山魈
gelada [dʒə'lɑːdə] [n] .... 狒狒
orangutan [ɔː,ræŋ uː'tæn] [n] .... 黑猩猩
rock-monkey [ph] .... 猕猴

Daily Q&A

〔会话一〕

Q▶ I am lost. I can't find my way home.
我迷路了，我找不到回家的路。

A▶ What you need is a compass. It can show you way home.
你需要一个指南针，它可以指出你回家的路。

〔会话二〕

Q▶ Ouch! I cut myself. It hurts.
噢！我割到自己了，好痛！

A▶ Let me check my first-aid kit. I can put a band aid on it.
让我看看我的急救箱，我可以在伤口上贴一个邦迪创可贴。

〔会话三〕

Q▶ Do you know how old this tree is?
你知道这棵树多少岁吗？

A▶ You can tell by its annual rings. One annual ring means one year.
你可以从它的年轮得知。一个年轮代表一岁。

Proverbs & Idioms 　**地道谚语与惯用语** | 让句子锦上添花

faith will move mountains　精诚所至，金石为开
Don't feel discouraged. Try again. Your faith will move the mountains.
不要气馁，再试一次。你将会精诚所至，金石为开。

If a mountain will not come to Mahomet, Mahomet must go to the mountain.
山不转自己转
You have a fight with your girlfriend? If your girlfriend doesn't call you, you need to call her first. If a mountain will not come to Mahomet, Mahomet must go to the mountain.
你和女朋友吵架了？如果你女朋友不打电话给你，你就要先打给她。你要山不转自己转。

make a mountain out of molehill　小题大做
It's not a big deal. Don't make a mountain out of molehill.
那没什么，别小题大做。

a mountain to climb　很难的事
Classifying the mountain-high garbage is a mountain to climb.
把像一座山那么高的垃圾分类是很难的事。

Money does not grow on the tree.　赚钱不容易
"Mom, can I have a computer?" "We can't afford that, you know. Money does not grow on the tree."
"妈，我可以买电脑吗？" "你知道的，我们负担不起。赚钱不容易。"

the top of the tree　登顶成功
Nobody would have guessed that Catherine could get to the top of the tree before her talented brother.
没有人想到凯瑟琳可以在她聪明的弟弟之前成功爬到顶端。

move mountains　竭尽全力
He loves her very much. He would move mountains for her.
他深爱着她。为了她，什么难事他都愿意做。

Unit 27 Go to a Farm 农场

Daily Conversation | 日常对话 | 模拟真实的日常对话

A Wow! This farm is huge and you can do many activities here.
哇,这个农场真的很大,你可以在这里做很多活动。

B That is true. Some people go camping; some people picking some fresh fruit; some people go boating and some people go grass skiing.
是真的。有些人露营,有些人摘新鲜的水果,有些人划船,还有些人滑草。

A I never knew there were so many fun things to do on a farm.
我从来不知道农场上有这么多好玩的事。

B Well, Let's go to the lake over there. Some people are fishing over there. I haven't had a chance to fish in a lake. I really want to try.
我们去那边的湖吧,有些人在那边钓鱼。我从来没有机会在湖里钓鱼,我真的很想试试。

A I think we need to buy some bait and borrow some fishing poles first.
我想我们需要先买一些饵,然后借一些钓竿。

B Yes, we can get what we need at the stands right by the lake. Who do you think will catch a big fish first?
对啊,我们可以在湖边的那些小摊子上买到那些东西。你觉得谁会先钓到鱼?

A Of course, I will.
当然,是我。

Additional Vocabulary & Phrases | 补充单词 & 短语

- **activity** [n] 活动
What's your favorite activity?
你最喜欢的活动是什么?

- **catch** [v] 捉
What did the cat catch?
猫捉到了什么?

Daily Sentences 高频用句 | 一分钟学一句，不怕不够用
07-08

- Where can I pick some apples*¹?
  我可以在哪里摘苹果呢？

- All the cows and sheep are kept in the pasture, so we can watch them just right by the fence.
  所有的牛和羊都被关在篱笆里，所以我们可以在篱笆旁边看它们。

- Is there anything I need to be aware of when I go horseback riding?
  我骑马时需要注意哪些事项？

- You should sit up straight and push your two thighs hard into the horse abdomen when riding a horse.
  你骑马的时候应该坐直并且用你的大腿夹紧马腹。

- Can we go boating in the lake?
  我们可以在湖上划船吗？

- There are many animal shows in the center of the farm. You can get the show schedule at the booth next to the farm and arrive there 10 minutes before the show starts.
  在农场中间有许多动物表演。你可以在农场旁取得表演时刻表，然后在每一场表演的前10分钟到达就可以了。

- We plan to go to the farm for vacation.
  我们计划到农场度假。

- We will have some recreation on the farm to enjoy our leisure time.
  我们会在农场做一些娱乐活动来享受我们的休闲时光。

★ 换个单词说说看 | 用单词丰富句子，让句子更漂亮！

Additional Vocabulary & Phrases | 补充单词 & 短语

- **aware** [a] 注意到、察觉到
  I wasn't aware that she's crying.
  我没有察觉到她在哭。

- **booth** [n] 小雅座
  We are going to meet at the booth in the restaurant.
  我们会在餐厅的雅座见面。

- **recreation** [n] 消遣、娱乐
  I like to do some recreation on the weekends.
  我喜欢在周末做些娱乐活动。

- **leisure** [a] 闲暇的
  What do you like to do in your leisure time?
  你在闲暇的时候喜欢做些什么？

Daily Vocabulary 语言学校都会教的实用日常单词
07-09

1 countryside 农村

ecology [ɪˈkɒlədʒi] [n]	生态
scenic spot [ph]	景点
farmer [ˈfɑːmə] [n]	农夫
farm [fɑːm] [n]	农场
field [fiːld] [n]	田野
farmhouse [ˈfɑːmhaʊs] [n]	农舍

2 domestic animals 家畜

sheep [ʃiːp] [n]	绵羊	cattle [ˈkætl] [n]	牛
lamb [læm] [n]	小羊	horse [hɔːs] [n]	马
cow [kaʊ] [n]	母牛		

3 turkey 火鸡

chicken [ˈtʃɪkɪn] [n]	鸡
goose [guːs] [n]	鹅
duck [dʌk] [n]	鸭
pigeon [ˈpɪdʒɪn] [n]	鸽子
rooster [ˈruːstə] [n]	公鸡
hen [hen] [n]	母鸡

4 crops 农作物

wheat [wiːt] n		小麦
barley ['bɑːli] n		大麦
maize [meɪz] n		玉米
rice [raɪs] n		水稻
buckwheat ['bʌkwiːt] n		荞麦
grain [ɡreɪn] n		谷物
sorghum ['sɔːɡəm] n		高粱
millet ['mɪlɪt] n		谷子

5 vegetable 蔬菜

tomato [təˈmɑːtəʊ] n		番茄
potato [pəˈteɪtəʊ] n		马铃薯
cabbage [ˈkæbɪdʒ] n		甘蓝
carrot [ˈkærət] n		胡萝卜
yam [jæm] n		红薯
pea [piː] n		豌豆
pumpkin [ˈpʌmpkɪn] n		南瓜

6 fruit 水果

strawberry [ˈstrɔːbəri] n		草莓
cherry [ˈtʃeri] n		樱桃
grape [ɡreɪp] n		葡萄
raspberry [ˈrɑːzbəri] n		覆盆子
apple [ˈæpl] n		苹果

7 flower 花卉

sunflower ['sʌnflaʊə] [n]	太阳花
rose [rəʊz] [n]	蔷薇
magnolia [mæg'nəʊliə] [n]	木兰花
coneflower ['kəʊn,flaʊə] [n]	雏菊
tulip ['tjuːlɪp] [n]	郁金香
lily ['lɪli] [n]	百合花
butterfly ['bʌtəflaɪ] [n]	蝴蝶

8 advance 发展

leisure ['leʒə] [n]	悠闲
vacation [və'keɪʃn] [n]	假期
recreation [,riːkri'eɪʃn] [n]	娱乐
observe [əb'zɜːv] [v]	观察
develop [dɪ'veləp] [v]	培养
experience [ɪk'spɪəriəns] [v]	体验
camp [kæmp] [n]	露营
grass skiing [ph]	滑草
horseback riding [ph]	骑马
archery ['ɑːtʃəri] [n]	射箭
fruit picking [ph]	采摘水果
go fishing [ph]	钓鱼
go boating [ph]	划船

Daily Q&A

〔会话一〕
Q▶ Can we buy some grass to feed the animals on the farm?
我可以买一些草喂农场里的动物吗？
A▶ Sure.
当然

〔会话二〕
Q▶ What animals can I see on the farm?
我在农场上可以看到哪些动物？
A▶ You can see lambs, cows and horses.
你可以看到绵羊、牛和马。

〔会话三〕
Q▶ What activities can I do on the farm?
我可以在农场上做哪些活动？
A▶ You can go fishing, grass skiing, camping, boating and horseback riding.
你可以钓鱼、滑草、露营、划船和骑马。

Proverbs & Idioms 地道谚语与惯用语 | 让句子锦上添花

farm someone out 把某人派去为他人工作
I have farmed my secretary out for a week, so I have to arrange all my appointments now.
我把我的秘书外派一周，所以我现在必须自己安排所有的行程。

farm something out 把某事发包给他人
We farm the packaging work out.
我们把包装发包给别人。

a funny farm 精神病医院
If things become worse, they will send me to a funny farm because they think my idea is really too crazy.
如果事情变得越来越糟了，他们将会把我送到精神病院，因为他们觉得我的主意实在是太疯狂了。

bet the farm 把所有的财产卖出来做其他的投资
It is not a wise idea to bet the farm on one investment.
把所有的财产集中在一项投资上，实在不是个聪明的主意。

factory farming 大量快速的农产制造
Due to the modern technology, a lot of food is produced by factory farming.
因为现代科技，很多食物在工厂里被大量制造。

don't put all your eggs in one basket 不要集中风险（要分散风险）
It's not good to put all your eggs in one basket. You need to cut risks, or you may lose everything.
把所有的鸡蛋放在同一个篮子里并不好。你要降低风险，否则你可能失去所有的东西。

make hay while the sun shines 要把握良机
When there is a great chance, just go for it. We should make hay while the sun shines. Stop spending time wondering.
如果有很好的机会来临，就去追求。我们要把握良机。不要花时间想结果。

pigs can fly 不可能的事
It's impossible for our boss to give us any more paid holidays. If he does, pigs can fly.
我们老板是不可能给我们更多的有薪假期的。他如果会这样做，猪都会飞。

Unit 28 Go to a Beach 海滩

Daily Conversation 日常对话 | 模拟真实的日常对话

A I can't wait to play in the water. My feet are burning when I stand on the sand.
我等不及去玩水了。我站在沙子上的时候，脚都快要烧起来了。

B I want to find a good place to enjoy the sunshine and get a perfect tan.
我想找一个好地方享受阳光并晒出好肤色。

A Did you bring the floats? I need one. I am not a good swimmer. I feel safer when I have them in the water.
你带游泳圈了吗？我需要，我不太会游泳。我带着它会比较安心。

B Don't worry. They are in the bag. Do you want to ride the jet ski?
不用担心，它们在带子里。你想骑水上摩托车吗？

A Sounds fun. Where can we rent it? Is it costly?
听起来很有趣，我们可以在哪里租到？很贵吗？

B Not at all.
一点也不贵

Additional Vocabulary & Phrases | 补充单词 & 短语

- **burn** [v] 发热、燃烧
  The house is burning.
  那栋房子烧起来了。

- **tan** [n] 棕褐色、晒成的棕褐的肤色
  I want to get some nice tan.
  我想要把我的皮肤晒成漂亮的棕褐色。

- **rent** [v] 出租、租用
  She rent a house in Taipei.
  她在台北租了一间房子。

- **costly** [a] 贵重的、昂贵的
  It is costly to spend a night at that luxury hotel.
  在那家奢华的酒店住一个晚上是非常昂贵的。

Daily Sentences 高频用句 | 一分钟学一句，不怕不够用

- What do we need when we go to the beach?
  我们去沙滩需要准备什么？

- I will need sunglasses, sunscreen, an ice box, water, hats, swimsuits, a towel and floats.
  我需要太阳镜、防晒霜、小冰箱、水、帽子、游泳衣、毛巾和游泳圈。

- It is safer not to swim in a deep water area.
  在深水区游泳是不安全的。

- Where can we rent a canoe *1?
  我们可以在哪里租到独木舟？

- Which one do you prefer, snorkeling or scuba diving?
  浮潜和潜水，你比较喜欢哪一个？

- The sun is scorching hot. Let's get some cold drinks.
  太阳很炙热，我们去买些冷饮吧。

- Put on your swim suit before swimming.
  游泳前，穿上你的泳装。

- I will bring a big hat and apply a lot of sunscreen before setting off to the beach.
  我会在出发去海滩前，戴一顶大帽子并涂很多防晒霜。

- What a lovely day. The sun is shinning and the sky is so blue. It's a perfect day to go to the beach and get a beautiful tan.
  今天天气真好。阳光普照，而且天空是如此蓝。这是个适合去海滩晒太阳的好日子。

- A sun tan symbolizes health and wealth in western countries.
  在西方国家中，晒太阳后的肤色象征着健康和财富。

★ 换个单词说说看 | 用单词丰富句子，让句子更漂亮！

Additional Vocabulary & Phrases | 补充单词 & 短语

- **safe** a 安全的
  You are safe here.
  你在这里是安全的。

- **scorch** v 把……烧焦、使枯萎
  The rose was scorched by the dreaded sun.
  炎炎烈日晒枯了玫瑰花。

Daily Vocabulary 语言学校都会教的实用日常单词
07-12

1 beachwear 海滩装

bathing suit [ph]	泳装
sunglasses ['sʌnglɑːsɪz] [n]	墨镜
bikini [bɪ'kiːni] [n]	比基尼泳装
hat [hæt] [n]	帽子
flip-flops [ph]	夹脚拖
diving suit [ph]	潜水衣

2 beachscape 海滩风光

sand [sænd] [n]	沙滩
sand castle [ph]	沙堡
sea [siː] [n]	海洋
bay [beɪ] [n]	湾
coast [kəʊst] [n]	沿海地区
billow ['bɪləʊ] [n]	巨浪、浪涛
wave [weɪv] [n]	波浪

3 shearwater 海鸥

palm tree [ph]	棕榈树	**beach umbrella** [ph]	海滩阳伞
seagull ['siːgʌl] [n]	海鸟	**relax** [rɪ'læks] [a]	放松的
beach chair [ph]	沙滩椅		

④ sailboat 帆船

tanker ['tæŋkə] [n]		油轮
boat [bəʊt] [n]		小船
speedboat ['spiːdbəʊt] [n]		快艇
canoe [kəˈnuː] [n]		独木舟
yachting [ˈjɒtɪŋ] [n]		游艇

⑤ lifeguard 救生员

security [sɪˈkjʊərəti] [n]		防御（措施）、防护
drown [draʊn] [v]		死
life jacket [ph]		救生衣
lifeboat [ˈlaɪfbəʊt] [n]		救生船
kickboard [ˈkɪkbɔːd] [n]		浮板
lifebuoy [ˈlaɪfbɔɪ] [n]		救生圈、救生带

⑥ seashell 贝壳

starfish [ˈstɑːfɪʃ] [n]		海星
sea dollar [ph]		沙钱
mussel [ˈmʌsl] [n]		蚌
hermit crab [ph]		寄居蟹
auger [ˈɔːgə] [n]		螺旋贝

7 scuba diving 水肺潜水

diver ['daɪvə] n		潜水员
sea turtle ph		海龟
clown fish ph		小丑鱼
sea anemone ph		海葵
coral reef ph		珊瑚礁
snorkeling ['snɔːklɪŋ] n		使用水下呼吸管潜游

8 surfing 冲浪

surfboard ['sɜːfbɔːd] n	冲浪板	beach volleyball ph		沙滩排球
beach ball ph	沙滩球	sunbathe ['sʌnbeɪð] n		日光浴
beach buggy ph	沙滩车	jet ski ph		水上摩托

Daily Q&A

〔会话一〕

Q ▶ How can you get a beautiful tan but not sunburn?
要怎么做，你才能让皮肤晒得漂亮又不会晒伤？

A ▶ **Just apply some sunscreen for tanning purpose.**
只要涂抹一些适合晒出漂亮肤色的防晒油就可以了。

〔会话二〕

Q ▶ People go surfing when the wave is big enough.
人们都在海浪够大的时候去冲浪。

A ▶ **Why?**
为什么？

〔会话三〕

Q ▶ Do you want to play beach volleyball?
你想要玩沙滩排球吗？

A ▶ **Why not?**
好啊。

Proverbs & Idioms 地道谚语与惯用语｜让句子锦上添花

not be the only pebble on the beach　成为次重要的人
Jeremy always expects to be the leader of everything. It is time for him to learn not to be the only pebble on the beach.
杰瑞米总是希望担任每件事的领导者。是时候让他学着当次重要的人了。

between the devil and the deep blue sea　两难的选择
I couldn't make up my mind. I was between the devil and the deep blue sea.
我没办法下定决心，我正面临一个两难的选择。

at sea　困惑
I can't understand at all. I am completely at sea.
我没办法了解，我完全困惑了。

sea change　重大的改变
There are too many on-going major plans this year. It is really not time for a sea change.
今年有太多正在进行的重大计划，实在不是个做重大改变的时机。

get one's sea legs　适应新生活
After moving to a new city, Jenny got her sea legs by starting her own business.
在搬去新城市之后，珍妮以开始她的事业来适应新生活。

boil the ocean　使海洋滚沸（不可能的事）
You're wasting my time. You might as well be boiling the ocean.
你在浪费我的时间。你可能在做不可能的事。

the coast is clear　没有危险
We had to wait until the coast was clear to get out of the building after the earthquake.
地震过后，我们必须等到没有危险时再走出这栋大楼。

Go to a Zoo 动物园

Daily Conversation 日常对话 | 模拟真实的日常对话

A Wow! This zoo is really huge.
哇！动物园真的好大。

B Yes, you can find hundreds of various animals here. It is the biggest zoo in Beijing.
是啊，你可以在这里看到数以百计不同种类的动物，这是北京最大的动物园。

A Look at the map. It has different areas, like the marine life, mammals, the polar animals and the insects.
看一下这张地图。动物园有好几个区，如海洋生物区、哺乳动物区、北极动物区和昆虫区。

B Where can we find the giraffes? I think we are here to see the giraffes.
我们可以在哪里找到长颈鹿呢？我想我们是来看长颈鹿的。

A We have to go to the mammal area. We are at the gate right now. We need to go straight from here and turn left and go along to the end and make another left turn.
我们必须到哺乳动物区。我们现在在大门这边，我们需要从这里直走、左转走到底，再左转。

B It will take at least 20 minutes to get there. Are there any shuttle buses?
听起来好像要花上至少 20 分钟才能到那里。动物园里有接驳车吗？

A Yes, there is one.
是的，有一辆。

Additional Vocabulary & Phrases | 补充单词 & 短语

- **huge** a 特大的
  This hamburger is huge.
  这个汉堡真的很大。

- **mammal** a 哺乳类动物
  Giraffes are mammals.
  长颈鹿是哺乳动物。

Daily Sentences 高频用句 | 一分钟学一句，不怕不够用

- Can I use the camera in the zoo?
  我在动物园里可以使用照相机吗？

- The flash will scare the animals.
  闪光灯会吓到动物。

- When you go on safari, remember not to get out of the car because you may be attacked by the wild tigers or lions.
  当你乘坐吉普车观赏野生动物时，记得不要下车，因为你可能会被老虎或狮子攻击。

- What do the pandas*1 eat?
  熊猫吃什么呢？

- We can take the shuttle bus provided by the zoo to go around places in the zoo.
  我们可以搭由动物园提供的接驳车在动物园中游览。

- You are not allowed to stick your hands through the bars. It is very dangerous. Some animals do attack people.
  你不能将手伸入笼子里，这非常危险，有些动物会攻击人的。

- Do not knock on the glass when you see fish in the tank.
  当你在水族箱看到鱼的时候，不要敲打玻璃。

- I would like to see the cute pandas*2.
  我想去看可爱的熊猫。

★ 换个单词说说看 | 用单词丰富句子，让句子更漂亮！

Additional Vocabulary & Phrases | 补充单词 & 短语

- **flash** n 闪光灯
  Can you turn off your flash?
  可以请你关掉闪光灯吗？

- **provide** v 提供
  They provided some free water.
  他们提供了一些免费的水。

- **allow** v 允许、准许
  I am not allowed to go out at night.
  我不被准许晚上出门。

- **knock** v 敲、击
  Please knock before you come in.
  进来请先敲门。

Daily Vocabulary 语言学校都会教的实用日常单词

1. Asian Animals 亚洲动物

panda ['pændə] [n]	熊猫
Malayan Tapir [ph]	马来貘
black bear [ph]	黑熊
Bengal Tiger [ph]	孟加拉虎
Asian Elephant [ph]	亚洲象

2. Australian animals 澳洲动物

kangaroo [ˌkæŋɡəˈruː] [n]	袋鼠
koala [kəʊˈɑːlə] [n]	考拉
Southern Cassowary [ph]	南方食火鸡
kiwi bird [ph]	奇异鸟
eastern gray kangaroo [ph]	灰袋鼠

3. livestock 家畜

pig [pɪg] [n]	猪	horse [hɔːs] [n]	马
dog [dɒg] [n]	狗	rooster [ˈruːstə] [n]	公鸡
cat [kæt] [n]	猫	cattle [ˈkætl] [n]	牛
rabbit [ˈræbɪt] [n]	兔子		

4 marine 海洋的

coral ['kɒrəl] [n] ⋯⋯⋯⋯⋯⋯⋯ 珊瑚
white whale [ph] ⋯⋯⋯⋯⋯⋯ 白鲸
dolphin ['dɒlfɪn] [n] ⋯⋯⋯⋯⋯ 海豚
walrus ['wɔːlrəs] [n] ⋯⋯⋯⋯⋯ 海象

sea turtle [ph] ⋯⋯⋯⋯⋯⋯⋯ 海龟
manatee ['mænətiː] [n] ⋯⋯⋯ 海牛
sea lion [ph] ⋯⋯⋯⋯⋯⋯⋯⋯ 海狮

5 flying animals 飞行动物

owl [aʊl] [n] ⋯⋯⋯⋯⋯⋯⋯⋯ 猫头鹰
bat [bæt] [n] ⋯⋯⋯⋯⋯⋯⋯⋯ 蝙蝠
mockingbird ['mɒkɪŋbɜːd] [ph] ⋯ 仿声鸟
dove [dʌv] [n] ⋯⋯⋯⋯⋯⋯⋯ 鸽子
hummingbird ['hʌmɪŋbɜːd] [n] ⋯ 蜂鸟

6 polar animals 极地动物

penguin ['peŋgwɪn] [n] ⋯⋯⋯ 企鹅
polar bear [ph] ⋯⋯⋯⋯⋯⋯⋯ 北极熊
seal [siːl] [n] ⋯⋯⋯⋯⋯⋯⋯⋯ 海豹
Arctic hare [ph] ⋯⋯⋯⋯⋯⋯ 北极兔

7 amphibian and reptiles 两栖爬虫动物

python ['paɪθən] [n] ········· 蟒蛇
snake [sneɪk] [n] ············ 蛇
turtle ['tɜːtl] [n] ············ 乌龟
lizard ['lɪzəd] [n] ············ 蜥蜴
chameleon [kə'miːliən] [n] ····· 变色龙

8 African animals 非洲动物

giraffe [dʒə'rɑːf] [n] ······ 长颈鹿		tiger ['taɪgə] [n] ········· 老虎	
elephant ['elɪfənt] [n] ····· 大象		gazelle [gə'zel] [n] ······· 羚羊	
zebra ['zebrə] [n] ·········· 斑马		camel ['kæml] [n] ·········· 骆驼	
leopard ['lepəd] [n] ········ 豹		ostrich ['ɒstrɪtʃ] [n] ····· 鸵鸟	
lion ['laɪən] [n] ··········· 狮子		bushbuck [bʊʃ'bʌk] [n] ····· 非洲羚羊	
chimpanzee [ˌtʃɪmpæn'ziː] [n] ····· 黑猩猩		rhinoceros [raɪ'nɒsərəs] [n] ····· 犀牛	
		hippo ['hɪpəʊ] [n] ·········· 河马	

Daily Q&A

〔会话一〕

Q▸ Who takes care of these animals in the zoo?
谁在动物园里照顾这些动物？

A▸ The zookeepers take good care of them.
动物管理员会照顾他们。

〔会话二〕

Q▸ Where can I get the zoo map?
我可以在哪里拿到动物园里的地图呢？

A▸ You can find it under the map signs in the zoo.
你可以在动物园里的导览地图牌下找到。

〔会话三〕

Q▸ Which area can I find the tigers?
我在哪个区可以看到老虎？

A▸ You can go to the mammal area.
你可以去哺乳动物区。

Proverbs & Idioms 地道谚语与惯用语 | 让句子锦上添花

a paper tiger 纸老虎
Will India make any changes? Or is it just a paper tiger?
印度会改变吗？还是只是个纸老虎？

as sly as a fox 像狐狸一般狡猾
Jack is as sly as a fox. He can think of a great idea in just a second.
杰克像狐狸一样狡猾，他可以一下子就想到一个好主意。

a bear hug 熊抱
Her boyfriend gave her an affectionate bear hug which almost took her breath away.
她的男朋友给她一个熊抱，让她几乎无法呼吸。

a dark horse 黑马
I didn't know Sue had written a book. She is a bit of a dark horse, isn't she?
我不知道苏已经写过一本书，她真是一匹黑马，不是吗？

have butterflies in one's stomach 胃里紧张的感觉
She always has butterflies in her stomach before a test.
考试前，她总是紧张到胃痛。

copycat 盲目模仿者
Melisa is such a copycat. First, she bought the same bicycle as me, and now she wants to go to the same school as me.
梅莉莎真是个盲目模仿者。首先，她买了一辆和我一模一样的自行车，然后，现在她想要和我上一样的学校。

dog days 狗日子（炎热的日子）
I often go swimming during the dog days in summer.
我在夏天炎热的日子里常常去游泳。

Everyday Sentences 语言学校独家传授的必备好句子

- Let's go see the pandas! The news said that two pandas arrived at the zoo last week.
  我们去看熊猫吧！新闻说上星期有两只熊猫被运到动物园。

- How can we get to the zoo ?
  我们要怎么去动物园呢？

- We can take the MRT and get off at the Zoo Station.
  我们可以搭轻轨在动物园站下车。

- If you insist getting to the African animal area on foot, I will keep my mouth shut.
  如果你坚持走路到非洲动物区，我会闭嘴的。

- Let's go to see the penguins after pandas. They are in the polar animal area.
  我们看完熊猫之后，去看企鹅吧，它们在极地动物区。

- If we are lucky enough, we can see the polar bear. It is right next to the penguins.
  如果我们够幸运的话，我们可以看到北极熊。它就在企鹅的旁边。

- Have you ever seen crocodiles, black widow spiders, scorpions, elephants and black bears?
  你有看过鳄鱼、黑寡妇蜘蛛、蝎子、大象和黑熊吗？

- What's your favorite animal?
  你最喜欢的动物是什么？

- I've never seen a polar bear.
  我从没有看过北极熊。

- That kangaroo is pregnant.
  那只袋鼠怀孕了。

MEMO

From AM-PM 从早到晚都用得到的必备好句子

- Your credit card is maxed out.
  您的卡已经刷爆了。

- Have you ever been to a KTV?
  你去过 KTV 吗？

- What is KTV?
  什么是 KTV？

- KTV is a place to sing karaoke.
  KTV 就是可以唱卡拉 OK 的地方。

- KTV is really popular in China.
  KTV 在中国很受欢迎。

- Could I have the receipt?
  可以给我收据吗？

- This price is more than I expected.
  这价格比我想得贵多了。

- It's time to get up.
  该起床了。

- I need to brush my teeth.
  我得刷牙了。

- I was in a rush this morning.
  我今早时间很赶。

- I need some time to brush my hair and put on make-up.
  我需要时间梳头和化妆。

MEMO

- I didn't sleep very well last night.
  我昨天晚上没睡好。

- Have some toast and eggs.
  吃一些吐司和蛋吧。

- I prefer drinking apple juice in the morning.
  早上我比较想喝苹果汁。

- Breakfast is the most important meal of the day.
  早餐是一天中最重要的一餐。

- What do you usually eat for breakfast?
  你早餐通常吃什么？

- What do you want for breakfast?
  你早餐想吃什么？

- Finish your breakfast in 5 minutes.
  5 分钟内吃完早餐。

- I'll give you ten more minutes.
  再给你 10 分钟。

- Can I have some ketchup, please?
  能给我些番茄酱吗？

- I'd like my steak medium-well.
  我的牛排要七分熟。

- The pepperoni pizza looks good.
  意大利肉肠比萨看起来很好吃。

MEMO

Chapter 8

Make-Over
改头换面打扮自己

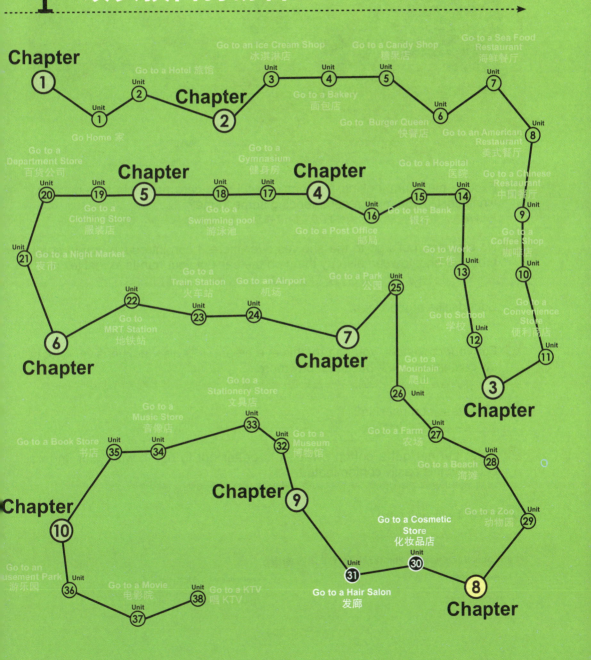

Unit 30 Go to a Cosmetic Store 化妆品店

Daily Conversation 日常对话 | 模拟真实的日常对话

A Excuse me. I am looking for some useful skin care products to reduce my wrinkles. Do you mind recommending some to me?
不好意思，我在找一些有用的去除皱纹的保养品。你能给我推荐一些不错的保养品吗？

B No problem. Let's go to the shelves over there. I can introduce you to some products and you can also try them on the back of your hands to feel texture.
没问题，我们去那一区。我可以介绍你一些产品，你也可以在手背上试试。

A Sounds like a good idea.
好主意。

B For your crowsfeet, you can try this eye cream. It is also inexpensive. A lot of my customers come back and buy more.
对于你的鱼尾纹，你可以试试这一瓶眼霜，它也不贵。我的很多顾客都会回过头再买一些。

A Can I test it on my skin?
我可以在我的皮肤上试吗？

B Sure. Let me get a cotton swab. It is better not to use it with your fingers because it is easily contaminated.
当然，我去拿一些棉花棒。你最好不要用你的手指，因为很容易弄脏。

A I see. I will wait here.
我了解，我会在这里等候。

Additional Vocabulary & Phrases | 补充单词 & 短语

- **wrinkle** [n] 皱纹
  He has some wrinkle on his face.
  他的脸上有一些皱纹。

- **contaminated** [a] 弄脏的、受污染的
  This glass of water is contaminated by the dust.
  这杯水被灰尘弄脏了。

Daily Sentences 高频用句 | 一分钟学一句，不怕不够用
08-02

- You can apply some eye cream around your eyes.
  你可以在眼睛周围涂一些眼霜。

- To have smoky eyes, you need a thick eyeliner. Use the eyeliner to draw line around your eyelids and smudge it gently.
  化烟熏妆时，你需要一只粗的眼线笔。用眼线笔在你的眼睑处画一条线，然后慢慢推开。

- To make your eyelashes look longer, you need a good mascara and an eyelash curler.
  想让眼睫毛看起来长一点，你需要一只好的睫毛膏和一个睫毛夹。

- My skin looks awful. What can I do?
  我的皮肤看起来真的很糟糕。我可以做什么？

- You can use a concealer to cover the dark circles around your eyes.
  你可以用一些遮瑕膏盖住你眼睛周围的黑眼圈。

- To have healthy skin, you need to use a makeup remover to completely remove all the makeup on your face.
  想要拥有健康的肌肤，你要用卸妆油彻底地卸掉脸上的妆。

- You need to do a facial treatment regularly. Then, you can try to put on some foundation to make your complexion look better.
  你需要定期做脸部护理，然后你可以试着涂一些粉底，让你的肤质看起来好一些。

- Can you recommend the latest lipstick *1?
  你可以介绍我最新款的口红吗？

★ 换个单词说说看 | 用单词丰富句子，让句子更漂亮！

Additional Vocabulary & Phrases | 补充单词 & 短语

- **thick** [a] 厚的、粗的
  This board is very thick.
  这块板子很厚。

- **smudge** [n] 污点、污迹
  There's a smudge on the wall.
  墙壁上有一个污点。

- **gently** [ad] 温柔地
  My girlfriend hold me gently.
  我女朋友温柔地抱着我。

- **awful** [a] 糟糕的
  His attitude was awful.
  他的态度非常糟糕。

205

Daily Vocabulary 语言学校都会教的实用日常单词
08-03

1 facial 脸部的

lip [lɪp] n		嘴唇
eyelid ['aɪlɪd] n		眼皮
cheek [tʃiːk] n		脸颊
skin [skɪn] n		皮肤
pore [pɔː] n		毛孔

2 clean 清洁

facial cleanser ph		洗面乳
make-up remover ph		卸妆油
foaming ['fəʊmɪŋ] n		泡沫慕斯
facial scrub ph		脸部磨砂膏
pore cleanser ph		去黑头

3 skin care 护肤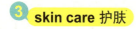

lotion ['ləʊʃn] n	护肤乳		nutrition [njuːˈtrɪʃn] n	滋养
moisturizer ['mɔɪstʃəraɪzə] n	保湿霜 / 乳 / 露		eye cream ph	眼霜
essence ['esns] n	精华液		astringent lotion ph	收敛水

206

④ mask 面膜

make-up base [ph]	隔离霜
sunscreen ['sʌnskriːn] [n]	防晒乳液
sun protection factor [ph]	防晒系数（SPF）
concealer [n]	遮瑕膏
lip balm [ph]	护唇膏

⑤ cosmetics 化妆品

foundation [faʊn'deɪʃn] [n]	粉底液
powder ['paʊdə] [n]	粉饼、蜜粉
mascara [mæ'skɑːrə] [n]	睫毛膏
eye liner [ph]	眼线笔
eye shadow [ph]	眼影
lipstick ['lɪpstɪk] [n]	口红
lip gloss ['lɪp glɒs] [ph]	唇蜜
blush [blʌʃ] [n]	腮红

⑥ mandelic acid 杏仁酸

hyaluronic acid [ph]	玻尿酸
laser resurfacing [ph]	激光除疤
intense pulsed light [ph]	脉冲光
chemical peeling [ph]	果酸换肤
botox injection [ph]	注射肉毒杆菌

7 makeover 美容

exfoliating [eksˈfəʊlieɪtɪŋ] v		去角质
revitalizing [ˌriːˈvaɪtəlaɪzɪŋ] v		活化
firming [fɜːmɪŋ] v		紧肤
whitening [ˈwaɪtənɪŋ] v		美白
detoxifying [ˌdiːˈtɒksɪfaɪŋ] v		排毒
refresh [rɪˈfreʃ] v		更新
acne [ˈækni] n		粉刺、青春痘

8 application 工具

eyelash curler ph	睫毛夹	**sponge puffs** ph		海绵扑
puff [pʌf] n	粉扑	**brow brush** ph		眉刷
brush [brʌʃ] n	刷子	**lip brush** ph		口红刷
tweezers [ˈtwiːzəz] n	拔毛钳	**cotton pads** ph		化妆棉
cotton swab ph	棉花棒	**eye shadow brush** ph		眼影刷

Daily Q&A

〔会话一〕

Q▶ Can you recommend me something useful for my scars?
你可以给我推荐一些有效去除疤痕的东西吗?

A▶ You should try this cream. It is good for scars.
你可以试试这个乳霜,它对疤痕很有用。

〔会话二〕

Q▶ I would like to put on some makeup before I go to the interview. I look pale.
我想在去面试前化点妆,我看起来很惨白。

A▶ You really should. It is also a kind of politeness.
你真的需要,而且化妆也是一种礼貌。

〔会话三〕

Q▶ I did not sleep well last night.
我昨天晚上真的没睡好。

A▶ I can tell from the dark circles around your eyes.
我可以从你眼睛周围的黑眼圈看得出来。

Proverbs & Idioms 地道谚语与惯用语｜让句子锦上添花

at first blush　第一眼、当下
At first blush, the room seemed to be perfect. However, we soon found there was no water and no electricity.
第一眼，那间房间看起来好像很完美。但是，我们很快就发现那里没水又没电。

save/spare someone's blushes　避免某人尴尬
The teacher saved the student's blush by scolding him in a private room with no one in it.
老师在一个隐秘没人的房间骂那个学生，以避免他会觉得尴尬。

the cream of the crop　最好的
These artists are the cream of the crop. All of them are very popular with people around the world.
这些艺术家都是最好的，他们全都是闻名世界的。

like the cat that got the cream　洋洋得意
Tim won the first prize of the lottery. He was sitting there and grinning like the cat that got the cream.
堤姆赢得了彩票头奖，他坐在那里笑得洋洋得意，令人讨厌。

someone's mask slips　摘下假面具
His mask suddenly slipped, and she saw him as a most terrible and ugliest man that he really was.
他突然摘下假面具，然后她看清楚了他真实的面貌是很丑陋又恐怖的。

Beauty is in the eye of the beholder.　情人眼里出西施
We have different ideas about beautiful girls. You know beauty is in the eye of beholder. Let's stop arguing who is right.
我们对漂亮女生有不同的看法。你知道情人眼里出西施吧。让我们不要再争谁对谁错了。

Beauty is only skin-deep.　美是件肤浅的事
I hate to upset you. Although Sandra is very beautiful, in her case, beauty is definitely only skin-deep. Her personality is terrible.
我不想让你失望。虽然桑德拉非常漂亮，就她而言美丽绝对是一件肤浅的事。她的个性很不好。

Unit 31 Go to a Hair Salon 发廊

Daily Conversation | 日常对话 | 模拟真实的日常对话

A So, how would you like your hair to be like?
那么，你想要剪什么样的发型？

B I want it to look more stylish. I would like it to be long still. But I want to have some fringe to cover my forehead.
我想要看起来比较有型。我希望我的头发还是长的，但是我想额头前有一些刘海。

A I got it. Do you want your hair to be straight, curly or wavy? I think you would look good with wavy hair.
我了解了。你想要留直发、卷发还是波浪卷？我想你很适合波浪卷。

B I have never tried to make my hair wavy. By the way, I want to color my hair.
我从来没有试过波浪卷头发。对了，还有，我想染发。

A Do you mean you want to dye your hair or just highlight it?
你的意思是说，要染全部还是挑染而已呢？

B Just highlight it.
挑染就好。

Additional Vocabulary & Phrases | 补充单词 & 短语

- **stylish** [a] 有型的
  Tom is very stylish.
  汤姆非常有型。

- **cover** [v] 覆盖、遮盖
  Can you cover your eyes?
  你能闭上你的眼睛吗？

- **forehead** [n] 额头
  She has a beautiful forehead.
  她的额头很漂亮。

- **highlight** [v] 使突出、强调
  Can you highlight this sentence?
  你能把这个句子强调出来吗？

Daily Sentences 高频用句 | 一分钟学一句，不怕不够用

- I use some hair spray to make my hair style last longer.
  我喷些定型液好让我的发型能维持得更持久。

- If you want to have curly hair, you need to perm it.
  如果你想拥有卷发，你需要烫。

- I have natural curls. I would like to straighten my hair.
  我有自然卷，我想把我的头发弄直。

- After washing your hair, it's better to apply some hair treatment to maintain the structure of your hair.
  洗发之后，最好抹上一些护发素，来保养头发的结构。

- I would like to tie my hair up with a pony tail in the back.
  我想要在脑勺后方绑一个马尾。

- I would like to leave my hair down to make me look more attractive.
  我要把头发放下来，让我看起来更有吸引力。

- Can you quickly use the hairdryer to dry my hair?
  你可以快速地用吹风机吹干我的头发吗？

- Can you braid *1 my hair?
  可以帮我编一下头发吗？

- Can you recommend a good hairdresser to me?
  你可以推荐我一个好的发型设计师吗？

★ 换个单词说说看 | 用单词丰富句子，让句子更漂亮！

braid *1 可以替换：

Additional Vocabulary & Phrases | 补充单词 & 短语

- **maintain** v 保持、维持、保养
  She maintains her piano very well.
  她把她的钢琴保养得很好。

- **structure** n 结构
  The structure of this article is very strong.
  这篇文章的结构很强。

- **tie** v 绑
  Can you tie my hair?
  你能帮我绑头发吗？

- **recommend** v 推荐
  Can you recommend me a nice hotel?
  你能推荐我一家好的饭店吗？

Daily Vocabulary 语言学校都会教的实用日常单词
08-06

1 hair 头发

long hair [ph]	长发
short hair [ph]	短发
medium hair [ph]	中长发
bangs [bæŋs] [n]	刘海
curly hair [ph]	卷发
straight hair [ph]	直发

2 hair salon 发廊

hair dresser [ph]	发型设计师
mirror ['mɪrə] [n]	镜子
salon chair [ph]	美发椅
designer assistant [ph]	设计师助理
design [dɪ'zaɪn] [v]	设计

3 shampoo 洗头、洗发水

conditioner [kən'dɪʃənə] [n]	护发素
hair spray [ph]	发型定型液
treatment ['triːtmənt] [n]	对待、治疗
essential hair oil [ph]	护发乳

4 tools 工具、器具、用具

scissors ['sɪzəz] n	剪刀
hair dryer ph	吹风机
hair clip ph	发夹
razor ['reɪzə] n	剃刀
rubber band ph	橡皮筋
hair curler ph	电棒卷
hair straightener ph	离子夹

5 technique 技术

procedure [prə'siːdʒə] n	程序
thinning ['θɪnɪŋ] v	打薄
wave [weɪv] n	（头发）波浪状；卷曲
layer ['leɪə] n	层次
straighten ['streɪtn] v	拉直
permanent ['pɜːmənənt] n	烫发
haircut ['heəkʌt] n	理发
dye [daɪ] n	染发

6 comb 梳子

wide tooth comb ph	宽齿梳
rat tail comb ph	扁平梳
barber comb ph	理发用梳
roller brush ph	圆梳
paddle brush ph	板梳

7 hairstyle 发型

afro [ˈæfrəʊ] n	爆炸头
crew cut ph	平头
bob [bɒb] n	鲍伯头
Pixie cut ph	精灵头
finger wave ph	手指波浪发

8 braids 发辫

ponytail [ˈpəʊniteɪl] n	马尾	crown braid ph	皇冠式发辫
pigtails [ˈpɪgteɪls] n	两个（马尾）	fishtail hair ph	鱼骨辫
French twist ph	法式发髻		

Daily Q&A

〔会话一〕
Q▶ How would you like to part your hair?
你想要怎么旁分你的头发？
A▶ I would like to part my hair on the left.
我想要左分。

〔会话二〕
Q▶ Would you like to dye your hair?
你想要染头发吗？
A▶ No, thanks.
不用，谢谢！

〔会话三〕
Q▶ How much is the shampoo?
这瓶洗发乳多少钱？
A▶ It's 1,000 dollars.
1 000 美元。

Proverbs & Idioms 地道谚语与惯用语 | 让句子更锦上添花

not have a hair out of place　一尘不染、看上去很干净
She is so tidy and clean. She does not have a hair out of place.
她是如此的整齐和干净，连头发都梳得整整齐齐，看起来很干净。

a bad hair day　不幸运的日子
It has been a bad hair day. My cell phone was not working when I talked to my girlfriend. I found my bike was stolen when I came back home.
今天真是个不幸的日子，我的手机在我和女朋友打电话时坏了；我回家的时候又发现，我的自行车被偷了。

hair-raising experience　恐怖的经验
Driving through the mountains is a hair-raising experience.
开山路真是个恐怖的经验。

not turn a hair　不受坏消息影响
I thought she would be furious. However, she did not turn a hair.
我本来以为她一定会很生气，但她丝毫不受坏消息影响。

put on a hair shirt　选择不享受乐趣来苦修
I don't think you need to put on a hair shirt in order to be a teacher. Life is short. You should do something more interesting and make yourself to feel happier.
我不认为老师只能严格地管理自己，而不能享乐。人生很短暂，应该做一些有趣而且快乐的事。

make one's hair stand on end　让人惊吓
Hearing the news about earthquakes made my hair stand on end.
听到关于地震的消息让我惊吓不已。

let your hair down　放轻松，做自己想做的事
The party gives you a chance to let your hair down at the end of the week.
这个派对是让你在周末放松心情做自己想做的事的一个机会。

gray hair　白头发
My grandmother is 78 years old now. She has a lot of gray hair.
我奶奶现在78岁了。她有很多白头发。

hang by a hair　薄弱的证据
Your whole argument is hanging by a hair.
你的整个论述证据薄弱。

Everyday Sentences　语言学校独家传授的必备好句子

- Your hair loses its style. You need to go to a hair salon. I can introduce my hair dresser to you.
  你的头发没有型了。你需要去发廊，我可以介绍我的发型设计师给你。

- Let's make an appointment first before we go there.
  在我们去那里之前，先预约一下。

- I am thinking about going to a hair salon. I look stupid with my hair like this.
  我正想去发廊。我头发这样看起来真的很呆。

- I was the one who made an appointment with Jimmy 30 minutes ago. My friend wants to change her hair style.
  我就是 30 分钟前和吉米预约的那个人。我的朋友想要改变她的发型。

- Welcome to ABC Hair Salon. Did you make an appointment with any of our hair dressers?
  欢迎来到 ABC 发廊，你们跟我们哪一位发型设计师预约了吗？

- I will bring you to your place.
  我会带你到座位上。

- I will sit on the sofa and wait for you here.
  我在这里坐在沙发上等你。

- If you dye you hair, you make all your hair in just one color. If you just highlight your hair, you just change part of your hair into a different color.
  如果你要全染，你把全部的头发变成单一的颜色；如果你只是挑染，你只把部分头发变成不一样的颜色。

- How long would you like your hair to be?
  你想要你的头发多长？

- In about one or two hours, you can see a whole new me.
  大概一到两个小时，你就会看到全新的我了。

- I would like my hair to be a little over shoulder.
  我想要我的头发过肩一点点。

From AM-PM 从早到晚都用得到的必备好句子

- How about getting some spaghetti with meatballs?
  来些意大利面配肉丸怎么样?

- What does the German sausage taste like?
  德国香肠吃起来味道怎么样?

- Cake is a nice dessert.
  蛋糕是很棒的甜点。

- The pie is too greasy.
  这馅饼太油了。

- The cookie is too sweet.
  这饼干太甜了。

- A lot of people come to this coffee shop to chat and drink coffee.
  很多人来这家咖啡店喝咖啡聊天。

- Don't waste your food.
  不要浪费食物。

- Vegetables are good for you. Eat more.
  蔬菜对你很好,多吃点。

- Thanks for cooking dinner, mom.
  妈,谢谢您做的晚餐。

- Would you please say grace for us?
  能请你帮我们做饭前祷告吗?

- Fast food is quick and cheap.
  快餐又快又便宜。

MEMO

- Eating too much fast food will make you fat.
  吃太多快餐会变胖。

- I'll order a cheeseburger with fries and Coke, please.
  我要点芝士汉堡、薯条和可乐，谢谢。

- This food is really greasy.
  这食物好油！

- The presentation of this dish is beautiful.
  这道料理的摆盘设计很漂亮。

- Do you eat sashimi?
  你吃生鱼片吗？

- What kind of meat do you want in your tepanyaki?
  你的铁板烧要什么肉？

- Could we have some more broths in the hot pot?
  能请你帮我们在锅里加点汤吗？

- Watch out! The soup is boiling.
  小心！汤开了！

- Do you want to try the spicy hot pot?
  你想试试麻辣火锅吗？

- Are you looking for a particular brand of shoes?
  你是在找特定品牌的鞋吗？

- Those are a nice pair of basketball shoes.
  那是双很不错的篮球鞋。

MEMO

Chapter 9
Art Enthusiast
知性文青

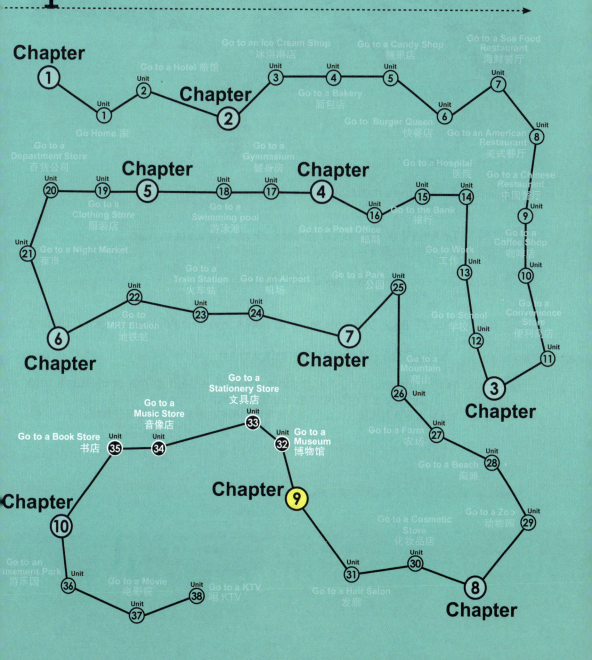

Unit 32 Go to a Museum 博物馆

Daily Conversation | 日常对话 | 模拟真实的日常对话

A Which floor is the art exhibition we are going to on?
我们要去艺术展的哪一层楼？

B I have no idea. Let me take a closer look at my museum map.
我不知道。让我仔细看看我的艺术馆地图。

A Sure, take your time. We have a whole day.
好，慢慢来。我们有一整天的时间。

B It's on the 2nd floor. We are going to see some beautiful paintings of ancient Greek.
在二楼。我们去那里看一些和古希腊有关的漂亮画作！

A Look at the museum guide. It says there are also some sculptures and potteries in this area. Let's rent an audio guide.
看看那个艺术馆导览！上面说在这里有一些雕像和陶器，我们去租个语音讲解吧！

Additional Vocabulary & Phrases | 补充单词 & 短语

- **map** [n] 地图
  I need a map.
  我需要一张地图。

- **whole** [a] 全部
  The whole class passed the exam.
  全班都通过了考试`。

- **ancient** [a] 古代的
  It is an ancient story.
  这是一个古老的故事。

- **pottery** [n] 陶器
  My grandma likes to collect potteries.
  我奶奶喜欢收集陶器。

Daily Sentences 高频用句 | 一分钟学一句，不怕不够用

- What exhibition is shown on the **ground floor** *¹?
  一楼有什么展览？

- This exhibition is about the **history** of **Spain** *².
  这是关于西班牙历史的展览。

- What is the **opening hours** of the museum?
  博物馆的开放时间是几点到几点？

- I would like to make a phone call to **enquire** about the museum. Do you have the number?
  我想打个电话到博物馆问一些信息。你有电话号码吗？

- The museum is open from 9 am to 7 pm every day.
  博物馆的开放时间是每天早上九点到下午七点。

- Every three to four hours, you can wait next to the information desk. A museum guide will tell you some **detailed** information about the exhibition.
  每三到四小时，你可以在询问台旁边等候，博物馆导览员会告诉你一些关于展览的详细信息。

- Excuse me, where can I find Monet's paintings in this museum?
  不好意思，我可以在这个博物馆的什么地方找到莫奈的画？

- Can I take photos here?
  我可以在这里照相吗？

★ 换个单词说说看 | 用单词丰富句子，让句子更漂亮！

Additional Vocabulary & Phrases | 补充单词 & 短语

- **history** [n] 历史
  My favorite subject is history.
  我最喜欢的科目是历史。

- **opening hour** [ph] 开放时间
  The opening hour of library is 7am-10pm.
  图书馆的开放时间是早上七点到晚上十点。

- **enquire** [v] 询问、查询
  I enquired about the graduate programs of Ohio State University.
  我询问了有关俄亥俄州立大学的硕士课程。

- **detail** [n] 细节
  He told me the details of the story.
  他告诉我那个故事的细节。

Daily Vocabulary 语言学校都会教的实用日常单词 09-03

1 topic 主题

science	['saɪəns] n	科学
history	['hɪstri] n	历史
astronomy	[ə'strɒnəmi] n	天文
humanity	[hju:'mænəti] n	人文
art	[ɑ:t] n	艺术
antique	[æn'ti:k] a	古代的
modern	['mɒdn] a	现代的

2 exhibition 展览

display	[dɪ'spleɪ] n	展示
period	['pɪəriəd] n	时代
memory	['meməri] n	纪念
on tour	ph	巡回的
hold	[həʊld] v	举办
preview	['pri:vju:] n	预告
review	[rɪ'vju:] n	回顾

3 visit 参观

audio guide	ph	语音讲解	ticket	['tɪkɪt] n	门票
handbook	['hændbʊk] n	手册	plan	[plæn] n	平面图
route	[ru:t] n	路线	introduction	[ˌɪntrə'dʌkʃn] n	介绍

4 hall 走廊

area [ˈeəriə] n		区域
audio-visual room ph		视听室
ticket booth ph		售票室
souvenir [ˌsuːvəˈnɪə(r)] n		纪念品

5 era 时代

renaissance [rɪˈneɪsns] n	文艺复兴时期
gothic [ˈɡɒθɪk] n	哥特式
Baroque [bəˈrɒk] n	巴洛克艺术
Rococo [rəˈkəʊkəʊ] n	洛可可式
Romanticism [rəʊˈmæntɪsɪzəm] n	浪漫主义
Impressionism [ɪmˈpreʃənɪzəm] n	印象派

6 artist 艺术家

Leonardo da Vinci n	达·芬奇
Raphael n	拉斐尔
Michelangelo n	米开朗琪罗
Millet n	米勒
Vincent van Gogh n	凡·高

7 collection 收藏品

sculpture	['skʌlptʃə] n	雕塑
pottery	['pɒtəri] n	陶器
copper	['kɒpə] n	铜制品
jade	[dʒeɪd] n	玉制品
classic	['klæsɪk] a	典藏的

8 painting 绘画

calligraphy	[kə'lɪgrəfi] n	书法	egg tempera	ph	蛋彩画
ink painting	ph	水墨画	mural painting	ph	壁画
oil painting	ph	油画	watercolor	['wɔːtəkʌlə] n	水彩

Daily Q&A

〔会话一〕

Q▶ How much do I need to pay for the entrance fee in this museum?
这家博物馆的门票要多少钱？

A▶ About 200 dollars.
大约 200 美元。

〔会话二〕

Q▶ Where can we rent an audio guide?
我们在哪里可以租到语音讲解？

A▶ It's at the desk next to the ticket booth.
在售票亭旁边的柜台。

〔会话三〕

Q▶ Do you know how to use the museum map?
你知道怎样看博物馆的地图吗？

A▶ It's easy. Just turn your map like this.
很简单，只要把地图转成这样。

Proverbs & Idioms 地道谚语与惯用语 | 让句子锦上添花

take a collection up from (sb.) for (sb. or sth.) 从某人那边募款给某人或某事
The teacher took a collection up from every student for the poor student who was not able to pay for his tuition.
老师从每个同学那里募款给无法交学费的穷苦学生。

make an exhibition of (oneself) 尽情表现
She is not only dancing but making an exhibition of herself in the public.
她不只跳舞，而且也尽情在大家面前表现自己。

be no oil painting 不吸引人
She has a very beautiful face but is no oil painting.
她有漂亮的脸蛋，但是一点都不吸引人。

history repeats itself 旧事重演
I think the two parties in that country are having fight again because history repeats itself.
我想那个国家的两个政党将会产生争执，因为旧事会一再重演。

museum piece 老（旧）式的东西
Look at the car over there! It is absolutely a museum piece.
看那边那辆车！它绝对是老东西。

make an exhibition of oneself 让自己出洋相
He is drunk. If he keeps drinking, he is going to end up making an exhibition of himself.
他喝醉了。如果让他继续喝酒，他最后会让自己出洋相。

Unit 33 Go to a Stationery Store 文具店

Daily Conversation | 日常对话 | 模拟真实的日常对话

A I have to go to shelf number 3 first to get my markers, color pencils, highlighters and some brushes.
我们必须先去三号架找我的马克笔、彩色笔、荧光笔和一些水彩笔。

B I also need some thumbtacks, whiteout and paper clips. Which shelf are they on? I can't find the number.
我需要一些图钉、修正液和回形针，它们在哪一个架上？我找不到号码。

A It's at the back. I think you are near-sighted. You had better get yourself a pair of nice glasses.
在后面，我想你近视了。你最好买一副好的眼镜。

B No, I am not near-sighted. I just did not notice it.
不，我没有近视，我只是没有发现。

A OK. Let's go to find the things separately and meet here again after 1 hour. Is that fine with you?
好，我们分头去找东西，一个小时后在这里碰面。你觉得这样好吗？

B That sounds like a perfect idea. We can save plenty of time.
听起来是个完美的点子，我们可以省很多时间。

Additional Vocabulary & Phrases | 补充单词 & 短语

- **near-sighted** [ph] 近视
  She is near-sighted.
  她近视了。

- **notice** [v] 注意
  Did you notice that she was crying?
  你注意到她在哭吗？

- **separately** [a] 分别地、个别地
  You need to wash the dishes separately.
  你要分开洗盘子。

- **plenty** [n] 充足、大量
  I have plenty of chocolate.
  我有很多巧克力。

Daily Sentences 高频用句 | 一分钟学一句，不怕不够用

- I need some notebooks, paper, whiteout, highlighters and pens.
  我需要一些笔记本、纸、修正液、荧光笔和钢笔。

- Where do you put **binder clips**★1?
  你们的装订夹放哪里？

- The notebooks are on the shelf next to the markers.
  笔记本在马克笔旁边的架子上。

- How many colors does this box of colored pencils have?
  这盒彩色铅笔最多有几个颜色？

- We ran out of pens. Let's go to the stationery store.
  我们的笔用完了，我们去文具店吧。

- Where is the nearest stationery store?
  最近的文具店在哪里？

- What time does the stationery store close?
  文具店几点关门？

- How much is a box of **ball point pens**★2?
  这一盒圆珠笔多少钱？

- We need to do a group report tomorrow. I need to go to the stationery store to buy something for the posters.
  我们明天要做小组报告，我要去文具店买一些做海报的东西。

★ 换个单词说说看 | 用单词丰富句子，让句子更漂亮！

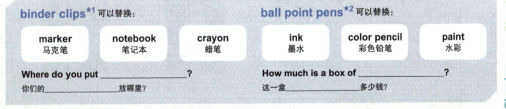

Additional Vocabulary & Phrases | 补充单词 & 短语

- near [a] 近的
  Sandy lives near my house.
  桑迪住在我家附近。

- poster [n] 海报
  This poster is well designed.
  这张海报设计得很好。

Daily Vocabulary 语言学校都会教的实用日常单词
09-06

1 paper 纸

card [kɑːd] [n]	卡片
sticky note [ph]	便利贴
memo pad [ph]	便条本
business card [ph]	名片卡
carbon paper [ph]	复写纸

2 tape 胶带

double-sided sticky tape [ph]	双面胶带
glue [gluː] [n]	胶水
glue stick [ph]	固体胶
acrylic foam tape [ph]	双面胶
scotch tape [ph]	透明胶

3 file 文件夹、公文箱

envelope ['envələup] [n]	信封	telephone directory [ph]	电话簿
letter paper [ph]	信笺	binder ['baɪndə] [n]	文件夹
folder ['fəuldə] [n]	文书夹		

④ ball point pen 原子笔

pencil ['pensl] n		铅笔
mechanical pencil ph		自动铅笔
fountain pen ph		钢笔
gel ink pen ph		中性笔
white out ph		修正液
eraser [ɪ'reɪzə] n		橡皮擦
mechanical pencil lead ph		自动铅笔笔芯

⑤ crayon 粉蜡笔

highlighter ['haɪlaɪtə] n		荧光笔
marker ['mɑːkə] n		马克笔
brush [brʌʃ] n		毛笔、画笔
watercolor ['wɔːtəkʌlə] n		水彩
complement ['kɒmplɪment] n		补充物
ink [ɪŋk] n		墨水、油墨

⑥ drafting 制图

ruler ['ruːlə] n		尺子
compass ['kʌmpəs] n		圆规
protractor [prə'træktə] n		量角器
setsquare ['setskwr] n		三角板

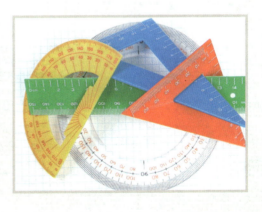

7 hardware 五金器具

scissors ['sɪzəz] n ······ 剪刀
blade [bleɪd] n ······ 刀片
craft knife ph ······ 美工刀

8 binder clips 装订夹

paper clips ph ······ 回形针
thumbtack ['θʌmtæk] n ······ 图钉
pin [pɪn] n ······ 大头针、别针
staples ['steɪplz] n ······ 订书针

9 business machine 事务机器

stapler ['steɪplə] n ······ 订书机
shredder ['ʃredə] n ······ 碎纸机
computer [kəm'pju:tə] n ······ 电脑
paper puncher ph ······ 打孔机
paper trimmer ph ······ 裁纸机
pencil sharpener ph ······ 削铅笔器

Daily Q&A

〔会话一〕

Q▶ Do you have any paper shredder?
你有碎纸机吗？

A▶ I am sorry. Our store does not sell any paper shredders.
对不起，我们的店没有碎纸机。

〔会话二〕

Q▶ How can I find everything on my shopping list in this store?
我怎么能在这家店找到我购物清单上的所有东西？

A▶ You can look at the signs on top of the shelves.
你可以看架上顶端的指示牌。

〔会话三〕

Q▶ Do you have any discount?
你们打折吗？

A▶ Yes, if you are our VIP member, you can get 20% discount.
是的，如果你是我们的VIP会员，你可以享有八折的优惠。

Proverbs & Idioms 地道谚语与惯用语 | 让句子锦上添花

be in the bull pen > 准备好回报他人

I am ready to be in the bull pen. Just call me whenever you need my help.
我准备好要报答你，只要你需要就打电话给我。

pen is mightier than the sword > 文字论述比武力战争有力

Believing that pen is mightier than the sword, the students decided to put what they were against in the newspapers instead of going on the street.
你要相信文字论述比武力战争更有力，那些学生决定把他们反对的事情登在报纸上，而不是走上街头。

a poison-pen letter > 恶意的匿名信

After the man was accused of laundering the money, his family soon received many poison-pen letters.
那个男人在被告洗钱之后，他的家人立刻收到很多恶意的匿名信。

put pen to paper > 付诸行动

Tim keeps thinking about writing to his dream lover, but he never puts pen to paper because he is afraid of being rejected.
提姆一直想写信给他的梦中情人，但是他从来没有付诸行动过，因为他很害怕被拒绝。

a pen pusher > 作家

He is a pen pusher who always dreams about traveling through the whole USA.
他是一个梦想旅游全美的作家。

glued to the spot > 被吓到不动了

Raymond stood there glued to the spot as the shadow of a thief came nearer and nearer.
当小偷的影子越来越逼近时，雷蒙被吓到不动了。

glued to something > （受到吸引）目光注视一处

During the football season, everyone's glued to the TV.
在足球季每个人的目光都盯在电视上。

Unit 34 Go to a Music Store 音像店

Daily Conversation 日常对话 | 模拟真实的日常对话

A This music store is really huge. You can find all kinds of CDs and tapes. If you want to learn how to play the musical instruments, you can also find a good one here.
这家音像店真大，你可以找到各式各样的 CD 和录音带。如果你想要学乐器，你也可以在这里找到一个好乐器。

B Wow, I can see **thousand**s of CDs and tapes on this side and on the other side I can see many different kinds of musical instruments **displayed** over there.
哇，我看到数以千计的 CD 和录音带陈列在这里，而在另一边，我看到不同种类的乐器。

A I love music. I always come here to buy the CDs I like because I can always find what I want.
我喜爱音乐。我总是来这里买我喜欢的 CD，因为我一定可以找到我要的。

B How can you find the CD you want to buy? I mean this store is really huge.
你怎么能够找到你想要买的 CD？我的意思是，这家音像店真的很大。

A Actually, it is not **difficult** at all. If you have the title, you can go to the counter and ask the counter helper to check whether they have it in the **stock**.
事实上，这一点也不难。如果你有唱片名，你可以去柜台，然后请柜台的人帮你查查有没有库存。

Additional Vocabulary & Phrases | 补充单词 & 短语

- **thousand** a 一千的
  Why do you always have thousands of questions?
  为什么你总是有好几千种问题？

- **display** v 陈列
  The cookies are displayed in the window.
  饼干陈列在橱窗里。

- **difficult** a 困难的
  It's difficult to learn a new language.
  学习一种新的语言是困难的。

- **stock** n 存货
  We still have many stocks.
  我们还有很多存货。

Daily Sentences 高频用句 | 一分钟学一句，不怕不够用
09-08

- How many people are there in this band?
  这个乐团有几个人？

- I am **looking for** a good piano. Can you recommend one to me?
  我想找一台好的钢琴，你可以给我推荐吗？

- Do you have the score of this music?
  你有这首音乐的乐谱吗？

- There are 5 people in this rock band, two vocalists, two drummers and a guitarist.
  这个摇滚乐队有五个人：两个主唱，两个鼓手和一个吉他手。

- Does this album come in tapes?
  这张专辑出过卡带吗？

- Are these CDs on special sale?
  这些 CD 有特别的折扣吗？

- Does your music store have a **website**?
  你们的唱片行有网站吗？

- Excuse me, I am looking for this CD. Do you have it in stock?
  不好意思，我在找这个 CD，你们有货吗？

- I like **classical music** *1.
  我喜欢古典音乐。

- I went to Super Junior's concert last night. It was fantastic.
  我昨晚去 Super Junior 的音乐会，真的很棒。

★ 换个单词说说看 | 用单词丰富句子，让句子更漂亮！

classical music*1 可以替换：

| country music | rock music | pop music | I like _____. |
| 乡村音乐 | 摇滚音乐 | 流行音乐 | 我喜欢_____。|

Additional Vocabulary & Phrases | 补充单词 & 短语

- look for [ph] 寻找
  I am looking for some yummy cheese.
  我在找一些好吃的芝士。

- website [n] 网站
  You can go on our website and order the products.
  你可以到我们的网站预订商品。

Daily Vocabulary 语言学校都会教的实用日常单词

① concert 音乐会
- **stage** [steɪdʒ] n. —— 舞台
- **show** [ʃəʊ] n. —— 表演
- **audience** [ˈɔːdiəns] n. —— 听众
- **spot light** ph. —— 聚光灯

② band 乐团
- **vocalist** [ˈvəʊkəlɪst] n. —— 主唱
- **keyboard player** ph. —— 键盘手
- **guitar player** ph. —— 吉他手
- **drummer** [ˈdrʌmə] n. —— 鼓手
- **bass player** ph. —— 贝斯手

③ chorus 合唱团
- **alto** [ˈæltəʊ] n. —— 中音部
- **soprano** [səˈprɑːnəʊ] n. —— 高音部
- **tenor** [ˈtenə] n. —— 次中音
- **bass** [beɪs] n. —— 低音部
- **choir** [ˈkwaɪə] n. —— 合唱

4 singer 歌手

lyricist ['lɪrɪsɪst] n		词作者
composer [kəm'pəʊzə] n		作曲者
lyrics ['lɪrɪk] n		歌词
score [skɔː] n		乐谱
recommend [ˌrekə'mend] v		推荐、介绍
popular ['pɒpjələ] a		大众化的
billboard ['bɪlbɔːd] n		排行榜
album ['ælbəm] n		专辑

5 orchestra 管弦乐器

instrument ['ɪnstrəmənt] n		乐器
piano [pi'ænəʊ] n		钢琴
flute [fluːt] n		长笛
trumpet ['trʌmpɪt] n		小号、喇叭
violin [ˌvaɪə'lɪn] n		小提琴
cello ['tʃeləʊ] n		大提琴

6 guitar 吉他

drum [drʌm] n		鼓
bass [beɪs] n		贝斯
keyboard ['kiːbɔːd] n		键盘乐器
electronic guitar ph		电吉他

7 audio 音响装置

compact disc [ph]	CD、唱片
tape [teɪp] [n]	卡带
earphone ['ɪəfəʊn] [n]	耳机
microphone ['maɪkrəfəʊn] [n]	扩音器、麦克风
MP3 player [ph]	MP3 播放器
CD player [ph]	CD 播放器

8 musical types 音乐类型

pop [pɒp] [n]	流行音乐	blues [bluːz] [n]	蓝调音乐
jazz [dʒæz] [n]	爵士乐	Britpop [n]	英式摇滚
rap music [n]	说唱音乐	folk music [ph]	民谣
classical music [ph]	古典乐	opera ['ɒprə] [n]	歌剧
electronic music [ph]	电子音乐	punk rock [ph]	朋客摇滚乐
rock-and-roll [ph]	摇滚乐		

Daily Q&A

〔会话一〕
Q▶ Is Super Junior's new album available now?
现在买得到 Super Junior 的新专辑吗?
A▶ Yes, you can find their CDs at the music store.
可以啊,你可以在音像店找到他们的 CD。

〔会话二〕
Q▶ I love this band a lot. They always make good rock and roll music.
我真的很喜欢这个乐队,他们总是可以创作出很好的摇滚乐。
A▶ Who is the vocalist? Who is the drummer?
主唱是谁? 鼓手是谁?

〔会话三〕
Q▶ What kind of music do you like?
你喜欢哪种音乐?
A▶ I like classical music.
我喜欢古典乐。

Proverbs & Idioms 地道谚语与惯用语 | 让句子锦上添花

face the music 面对现实
Not being able to be accepted by the school is a fact. You should face the music.
没被学校录取的事实，你要面对现实。

make chin music 说话
Jim loves talking. He will make hours of chin music to let everyone listen to him.
吉姆很爱说话，他会让别人听他讲几小时的话。

music to someone's ears 令人悦耳的话
A: You look so beautiful tonight.
A: 你今天看起来真漂亮。
B: Ah, that is music to my ears.
B: 哈，这真是令人悦耳的话。

preach to the choir 在已认同你的人面前阐述自己的言论
I finally realized that all I was doing was preaching to the choir. The men who really needed to hear this did not come.
我最后了解到，我所做的都是在已经认同我的人面前说服他们，真的需要被说服的人却都没来听。

jazz something up 使有型、使有趣
Mom, you need to jazz up your wardrobe. All your clothes are old fashioned.
妈妈，你要让你的衣橱有更多有型的衣服，你的衣服都很老气。

strike a false note 做错的或是不合时宜的事
David found out that he struck a false note when he arrived at the theme party with wrong dress code.
当大卫穿错衣服参加主题派对时，他发现他做了件不合时宜的事。

ring a bell 熟悉的事
Melisa? The name rings a bell but I don't remember her.
梅丽莎？这名字好熟悉，但是我想不起来她是谁。

Unit 35 Go to a Bookstore 书店

Daily Conversation 日常对话 | 模拟真实的日常对话

A Excuse me, Ma'am. I am looking for books about business. Where is the business **section**?
不好意思，女士。我们在找商业相关的书，商业书籍区在哪里？

B Go straight and turn left. It's next to the computer section. If you know the **title** of the book, I can **search** the book for you on the Internet.
直走左转，它在电脑区的旁边。如果你知道书名，我可以在网上替你查询。

A OK. I think I will look around first.
好，我会先到处看看。

B Just tell me when you need my help.
有需要时就叫我。

A No problem. Thank you very much.
没问题，谢谢你。

B You're welcome. It's my **pleasure**.
不客气，这是我的荣幸。

Additional Vocabulary & Phrases | 补充单词 & 短语

- **title** [n] 标题、书名
  What's the title of the book?
  那本书的书名是什么？

- **search** [v] 搜查、搜寻
  What are you searching for?
  你在找什么？

- **pleasure** [n] 愉快、高兴、满足
  It is such a pleasure to spend time with you.
  花时间和你相处真的很愉快。

Daily Sentences 高频用句 | 一分钟学一句，不怕不够用

- I would like to find books about literature. Where are they?
  我想找文学相关的书籍，它们在哪里？

- Language learning books are next to the literature section down the <mark>aisle</mark>.
  语言工具书在过道 / 走廊 / 通道尽头的文学书籍区的旁边。

- Can you <mark>check</mark> whether you have this book in your shop or not?
  你可以帮我找找你们店里有这本书吗？

- What's the book title and the writer's name?
  这本书的书名和作者是谁？

- Do you know any good bookstore in this <mark>neighborhood</mark>?
  你知道这附近有好的书店吗？

- There is a big bookstore in Taipei 101. You can find a lot of <mark>interesting</mark> books there.
  台北 101 里有一家大的书店，你可以在那里找到很多有趣的书。

- How much money do you spend on books every year?
  你每年花多少钱买书？

- What kinds of books interest you?
  你对哪种书有兴趣？

- I would like to get a **map** *1 at a bookstore.
  我要在书店买一张地图。

★ 换个单词说说看 | 用单词丰富句子，让句子更漂亮！

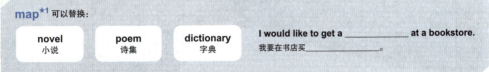

Additional Vocabulary & Phrases | 补充单词 & 短语

- **aisle** [n] 走道
  Dictionaries are located at aisle number 2.
  字典在第二走道。

- **check** [v] 检查、核对
  Can you check this list for me?
  你能帮我核对这张清单吗？

- **neighborhood** [n] 邻近地区
  Sandy lives around our neighborhood.
  桑迪住在我们家附近。

- **interesting** [a] 有趣的
  This book is very interesting.
  这本书很有趣。

Daily Vocabulary 语言学校都会教的实用日常单词
09-12

1 magazine 杂志

periodical	[ˌpɪəriˈɒdɪkl] [n]	期刊
sketchbook	[ˈsketʃbʊk] [n]	绘本
comic	[ˈkɒmɪk] [n]	漫画
newspaper	[ˈnjuːzpeɪpə] [n]	报纸

2 genre 文学类型

poem	[ˈpəʊɪm] [n]	诗
novel	[ˈnɒvl] [n]	小说
drama	[ˈdrɑːmə] [n]	戏剧
short story	[ph]	短篇小说
myth	[mɪθ] [n]	神话
graphic novel	[ph]	连环画小说

3 language 语言

simplified Chinese	[ph]	简体字	English	[ˈɪŋglɪʃ] [n]	英语
foreign language	[ph]	外文	Chinese	[ˌtʃaɪˈniːz] [n]	中文
Japanese	[ˌdʒæpəˈniːz] [n]	日语	dictionary	[ˈdɪkʃənri] [n]	字典

4 writer 作家

novelist ['nɒvəlɪst] [n] 小说家
poet ['pəʊɪt] [n] 诗人
masterpiece ['mɑːstəpiːs] [n] 名著
translator [trænsˈleɪtə] [n] 译者
manuscript [ˈmænjuskrɪpt] [n] 手稿

5 bookstore 书局

check-out counter [ph] 工作台
bestseller [n] 畅销书作家
borrow [ˈbɒrəʊ] [v] 借
return [rɪˈtɜːn] [v] 归还
storage [ˈstɔːrɪdʒ] [n] 仓库
check [tʃek] [v] 盘点

6 publisher 出版社

editor [ˈedɪtə] [n] 编辑
marketing [ˈmɑːkɪtɪŋ] [n] 销售
publishing [ˈpʌblɪʃɪŋ] [n] 出版
copyright [ˈkɒpiraɪt] [n] 版权
royalty [ˈrɔɪəlti] [n] 版税

7 book binding 装订

hardcover [ph]		精装书
paperback ['peɪpəbæk] [n]		平装书
bookmark ['bʊkmɑːk] [n]		书签
perfect binding [ph]		胶订书
second-hand book [ph]		二手书

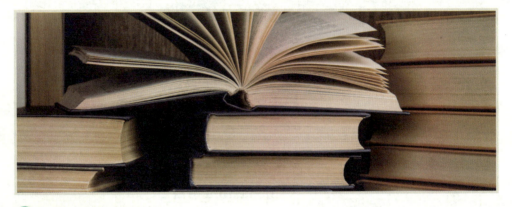

8 category 种类

business ['bɪznɪs] [n]		商业	architecture ['ɑːkɪtektʃə] [n]		建筑
philosophy [fə'lɒsəfi] [n]		哲学	education [,edʒu'keɪʃn] [n]		教育
social ['səʊʃl] [n]		社会	literature ['lɪtrətʃə] [n]		文学
psychology [saɪ'kɒlədʒi] [n]		心理	computer [kəm'pjuːtə] [n]		电脑
design [dɪ'zaɪn] [v]		设计	photography [fə'tɒgrəfi] [n]		摄影
cooking ['kʊkɪŋ] [n]		烹饪	politics ['pɒlətɪks] [n]		政治

Daily Q&A

〔会话一〕
Q▶ Do you have this book in English version?
你有这本书的英文版吗？
A▶ Let me check. Yes, it is in front of the check-out counter.
让我查一查。有，它在结账柜台前。

〔会话二〕
Q▶ Can you recommend me a good philosophy book?
你可以推荐给我一本好的哲学书吗？
A▶ Sure. *Sophie's World* is a good book.
当然，《苏菲的世界》是本好书。

〔会话三〕
Q▶ Excuse me. On which floor is the bookstore?
不好意思，书店在哪一楼？
A▶ It's on the 10th floor.
在十楼。

Proverbs & Idioms 地道谚语与惯用语 | 让句子锦上添花

cook the book 记假账
The accountant had been cooking the book. Our company had been losing money because of that.
那个会计一直都在做假账，我们的公司之前因为这样损失了不少钱。

be an open book 率直的人
Tina is an open book, so you will know right away if she does not like something or someone.
缇娜是个很率直的人，如果她不喜欢某件事或某人，你可以马上就能知道。

cuddle up with a book 曲着身体认真地阅读一本书
In my free time, I like to cuddle up with a good book.
在我有空的时候，我喜欢蜷缩着身体认真地看一本书。

crack a book 打开书
Kevin failed his test because he seldom cracked his book.
凯文考试不及格，因为他很少看书。

have a nose in a book 埋首苦读
Sam always has his nose in a book whenever I see him. He never does any exercise.
每次我看到山姆的时候，他都埋首苦读。他很少运动。

every trick in the book 用尽所有方法
He used every trick in the book to reach his goal. He does not care about whether he is honest. What he really cares is to win in every game.
他用尽所有的方法达到他的目标，他从不在乎他是否诚实，他只在乎赢得每一场游戏。

don't / never judge a book by its cover 不要以貌取人
Jenny looks a bit sloppy, but don't judge a book by its cover. She is the smartest student at her school.
珍妮看起来有些邋遢，但是不要以貌取人。她是全校最聪明的学生。

take a page out from someone's book 模仿、仿效
Many modern inventors took a page from Edison's book and began inventing useful little things.
现在很多发明家都仿效爱迪生并且研发出很多实用的东西。

Everyday Sentences 语言学校独家传授的必备好句子

- I need to buy some books. Do you want to go to the bookstore with me?
  我需要买一些书，你要跟我一起去书店吗？

- I need to do a report about business. I want to find some books that I can apply some of the ideas in them.
  我要做一篇商业的报告，我想找一些我可以采用里面好建议的书。

- I think I can read some comics and novels there while you are searching for your book.
  我想我可以在你找书的时候，看一些漫画和小说。

- I am free today. I can go with you to the bookstore. What kinds of books do you want to buy?
  我今天有空。我可以跟你一起去书店。你想要买哪一种书？

- The clerk is very helpful and friendly. She wears a sweet smile all the time.
  那位店员很愿意帮忙，并且很友善。她总是带着甜甜的微笑。

- I will read my comic books and novels there. When you are ready to go home, just come and find me.
  我会先在那里看我的漫画和小说，你要回家的时候就来找我。

- What's your favorite book?
  你最喜欢哪本书？

- Who's your favorite author?
  你最喜欢的作家是谁？

- Have you heard of *Fifty shades of Grey*?
  你听过《五十度灰》吗？

- Ellen DeGeneres is one of the most famous bestsellers.
  艾伦・德杰尼勒斯是最有名的畅销作家之一。

- Mitch Albom is one of my favorite authors.
  米奇・艾尔邦是我最喜欢的作家之一。

MEMO

From AM-PM 从早到晚都用得到的必备好句子

- They're too expensive.
  它们太贵了。

- High heels give me blisters.
  高跟鞋让我的脚起水泡。

- $30 is too much. How about $20?
  30美元太贵了，20美元如何？

- You should always try to bargain for a better price.
  你每次都应该试着杀价来获取便宜一点的价钱。

- How much are these?
  这些多少钱？

- What's the price after the discount?
  打折后是多少？

- You can count sheep if you cannot fall asleep.
  如果你睡不着可以数羊。

- I've been lying in bed for an hour.
  我已经躺在床上一小时了。

- It's three in the morning and I still can't fall asleep.
  已经凌晨三点了，我还不能入睡。

- I haven't been able to fall asleep for days.
  我已经好多天睡不着了。

- Would you like to have a cup of coffee?
  你想要来一杯咖啡吗？

MEMO

- I would prefer a cup of tea.
  我想喝一杯茶。

- I would like to have a piece of cake.
  我想吃一块蛋糕。

- I'd like a large latte.
  我要一杯大杯拿铁。

- Can I have a small mocha, please?
  一杯小杯摩卡，谢谢。

- Could you give me a packet of sugar with my coffee?
  你能给我的咖啡加一包糖吗？

- I'd like a cup of black coffee.
  我想要一杯黑咖啡。

- Let's play basketball in the park.
  我们去公园打篮球吧！

- I enjoy watching baseball on TV.
  我喜欢看棒球电视转播。

- How long does it take for you to go home?
  你回家要多久？

- I'm in a rush to get back home today.
  我今天赶着要回家。

- It's time for dinner!
  晚餐时间到！

MEMO

Chapter 10

Entertainment
放松娱乐一下

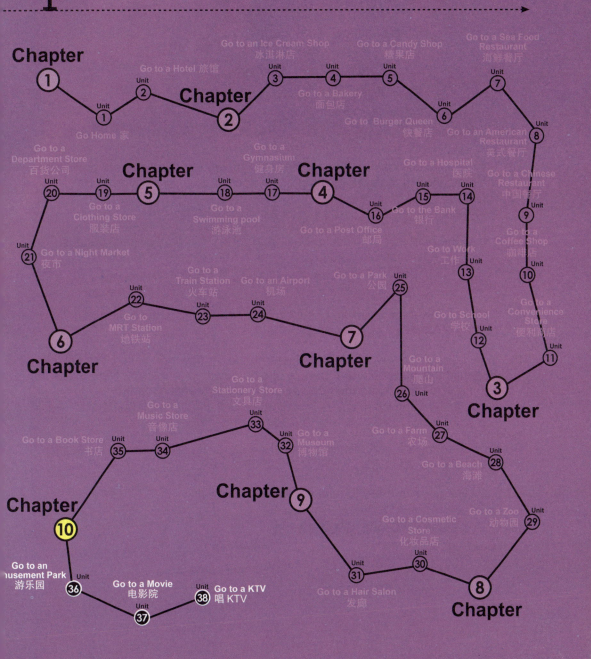

Unit 36 Go to an Amusement Park 游乐园

Daily Conversation | 日常对话 | 模拟真实的日常对话

A I love the roller coaster. It is my favorite ride in every amusement park. I love the sensation of the wind blowing on my face. It is really exciting.
我最喜欢坐过山车了，那是我在每一个游乐园里头的最爱。我喜欢风吹过脸颊时的兴奋感，真的很刺激。

B I love the pirate boat. It rocks back and forth. It is pretty scary because the only thing you can hold onto is just a bar in front of you.
我最爱海盗船，它往前又往后摇，实在可怕，因为你唯一可以抓住的东西只有你前面的那根杆子。

A Do you know if there are any new exciting rides in this amusement park?
你知道这家游乐园里有新的、刺激的游乐设施吗？

B Yup, there are a few. My friend recommended a new ride called The Oil Well. She said the well could turn people upside down up in the sky. Nine out of ten people who have taken the ride can't help but screaming loudly.
是的，有一些。我的朋友给我介绍了一个新的游乐设施，叫做老油井，她说那个老油井可以把人们倒吊在空中，玩过的人，十个有九个都会忍不住尖叫。

A Wow. That sounds really attractive to me. How can I miss taking such an exciting ride?
哇！听起来好吸引人，我怎么能错过这么刺激的游乐设施呢？

B Let's line up over there to take the roller coaster frist.
我们先排队去玩那个过山车吧！

Additional Vocabulary & Phrases | 补充单词 & 短语

- **sensation** n 感觉、知觉
Cotton candy gives a sensation of tender.
棉花糖给人一种柔软的感觉

- **wind** n 风
The wind is so strong today.
今天刮的风很强。

- **pirate** n 海盗
The pirate robbed the passengers.
那群海盗抢劫那些旅客。

- **scream** v 尖叫
Please don't scream at the bookstore.
在书店请不要大声尖叫。

Daily Sentences 高频用句 | 一分钟学一句，不怕不够用

- Where can we buy tickets for the amusement park?
  我们在哪里可以买到游乐园的票呢？

- Where is the **Merry-Go-Round**^{*1}?
  旋转木马在哪里？

- Are there any food **vendors**?
  这里有卖食物的摊贩吗？

- You can buy it at the booth in front of the gate.
  你可以在大门前的售票亭买到。

- I would like to buy some **souvenirs.** Can you show me how to get to the souvenir shop from here?
  我想买一些纪念品，你可以告诉我怎么从这里到纪念品商店吗？

- What is your favorite ride in an amusement park?
  游乐园里你最喜欢的游乐设施是什么？

- Can you recommend some interesting rides in an amusement park to us?
  你可以推荐我一些游乐园里有趣的游乐设施吗？

- I do not like the **haunted** house because it is **fake** and is not scary at all.
  我不喜欢鬼屋，因为它好假，而且一点都不可怕。

- I am thirsty. I see a food vendor over there. Let's go buy something to drink after riding the roller coaster.
  我好渴。我看到那里有一些卖食物的摊贩，我们玩了过山车后，去买些东西来喝吧！

★ 换个单词说说看 | 用单词丰富句子，让句子更漂亮！

Merry-Go-Round^{*1} 可以替换：

roller coaster	pirate boat	haunted house
过山车	海盗船	鬼屋

Where is the _____?
_____ 在哪里？

Additional Vocabulary & Phrases | 补充单词 & 短语

- **vendor** [n] 小贩、叫卖者
  Are there any candy vendors in the amusement park?
  游乐园里面有卖糖果的小贩吗？

- **souvenir** [n] 纪念品
  I want to buy some souvenirs for my girlfriend.
  我想给我女友买些纪念品。

- **haunted** [a] 闹鬼的
  This house is said to be haunted.
  传说这栋房子闹鬼。

- **fake** [a] 假的、冒充
  This is just a fake doll.
  这只是一个假娃娃。

Daily Vocabulary 语言学校都会教的实用日常单词

1 ticket window 售票口

ticket	['tɪkɪt]	n	入场券
adult	['ædʌlt]	n	成人
child	[tʃaɪld]	n	小孩
disabled	[dɪs'eɪbld]	a	残障的
group	[gruːp]	n	团体
teenager	['tiːneɪdʒə]	n	青少年
free	[friː]	a	免费

2 cotton candy 棉花糖

lollipop	['lɒlipɒp]	n	棒棒糖
popsicle	['pɒpsɪkl]	n	冰棒
ice cream sandwich		ph	冰淇淋三明治
hot dog		ph	热狗
ice cream cone		ph	冰淇淋甜筒

3 amusement 娱乐

funny	['fʌni]	a	有趣的
exciting	[ɪk'saɪtɪŋ]	a	刺激、使兴奋
happy	['hæpi]	a	快乐的
enjoyable	[ɪn'dʒɔɪəbl]	a	享受的
joyful	['dʒɔɪfl]	a	充满喜悦的
horror	['hɒrə]	a	恐怖的
scary	['skeəri]	a	惊吓的

4 theme 主题

water park [ph]	水上乐园
land park [ph]	陆上乐园
fantasy land [ph]	奇幻世界
magic kingdom [ph]	魔法王国
animal kingdom [ph]	动物王国

5 castle 城堡

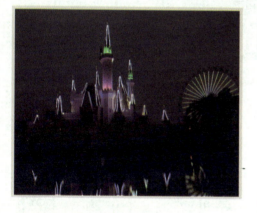

princess [ˌprɪnˈses] [n]	公主
prince [prɪns] [n]	王子
king [kɪŋ] [n]	国王
queen [kwiːn] [n]	皇后
crown [kraʊn] [n]	皇冠
fireworks [ˈfaɪəwɜːks] [n]	烟火

6 safari 非洲狩猎

jeep [dʒiːp] [n]	吉普车
desert [ˈdezət] [n]	沙漠
jungle [ˈdʒʌŋgl] [n]	丛林
giraffe [dʒəˈrɑːf] [n]	长颈鹿
lion [ˈlaɪən] [n]	狮子

7 pay attention 注意

maintenance	['meɪntənəns] [n]	维修、保养
restrict	[rɪ'strɪkt] [v]	限制
forbid	[fə'bɪd] [v]	禁止
pause	[pɔːz] [n]	暂停
emergency	[i'mɜːdʒənsi] [n]	紧急情况
cooperation	[kəʊˌɒpə'reɪʃn] [n]	合作
heart attack	[ph]	心脏病

8 facility 设施

merry-go-round	['meri gəʊ raʊnd] [n]	旋转木马
roller coaster	[ph]	过山车
bumper car	[ph]	碰碰车
ferris wheel	[ph]	摩天轮
go-kart	[ph]	赛车
pirate ship	[ph]	海盗船
haunted house	[ph]	鬼屋
shuttle train	[ph]	游园火车
great fall	[ph]	大瀑布
octopus	['ɒktəpəs] [n]	章鱼转
raft	[rɑːft] [n]	橡皮艇

Daily Q&A

〔会话一〕
Q▶ Where is the entrance of the ride?
这个游乐设施的入口在哪里？

A▶ It's near the small wooden booth over there.
在靠近那里的一座木制小售票亭。

〔会话二〕
Q▶ Where is the exit of the ride?
那个游乐设施的出口在哪里？

A▶ Follow the sign, and you can find the way to go out.
跟着标示走，你可以找到出去的路。

〔会话三〕
Q▶ The lines are long.
那排队伍真长。

A▶ Yup, we will have to wait more than 30 minutes.
是的，我们至少要等超过30分钟。

Proverbs & Idioms 地道谚语与惯用语 | 让句子锦上添花

a bumpy ride 不好的时机
The construction industry is in for a bumpy ride next year.
明年是营造业时机不好的一年。

ride a wave of (something) 受到……爱戴
The candidate rides a wave of good feelings among voters that makes him unlikely to lose the election.
候选人受到选民的爱戴，他不可能输掉这场选战。

free ride 搭便车
I got a free ride from Jack last week.
我上一周搭了杰克的便车。

thumb a ride 做出搭便车的手势
My car broke down on the highway, and I have to thumb a ride to get back to Taipei.
我的车在高速公路上坏了，所以我做出搭便车的手势，搭便车到台北。

if two ride on a horse, one must ride behind
一山难容二虎，需要有一方妥协
We can only decide to do one thing when we need to work together. If two ride a horse, one must ride behind.
当我们一起工作时，我们只能决定一件事情。一山难容二虎，需要有一方妥协。

a level playing field 公平的状态
People call for new rules in order to allow them to compete on a level playing field with other football teams.
人们要求新的规则让他们和其他的足球队公平竞赛。

foul play 不正当的手段
A virus wiped out all our computer-held records. We suspect foul play on the part of an ex-employee.
病毒清除了我们公司所有电脑的档案。我们怀疑这是之前的员工进行的破坏。

Go to a Movie 电影院

Daily Conversation | 日常对话 | 模拟真实的日常对话

A There are many new movies coming out this week. Let me look at the movie schedule and see when the earliest show is.
这一周有很多新电影上映。让我看一下电影时刻表，然后看一下离现在最接近的场次是什么时候。

B I have checked it online. I think it is the one at 6:30 pm.
我在网上查过了，我想是六点半那一场。

A It's 6:40 pm. We are late for the movie. I think it is better for us to see the next show.
现在已经六点四十，我们已经迟到了。我想我们最好看下一场。

B We can still see that one since trailers at the beginning of the movies usually take about 20 minutes. In this case, we are still on time.
我们可以看这一场，因为每场电影前的预告片通常都会有20分钟长。依照这个惯例，我们还是能准时看到这场电影。

A You are right. How come I did not think of this?
你说得对，我怎么没有想到呢？

B Well, two heads are always better than one. Let's go into the movie theater now.
嗯，三个臭皮匠胜过一个诸葛亮。我们赶快进电影院吧！

Additional Vocabulary & Phrases | 补充单词 & 短语

- **come out** [ph] （电影）上映
  Fifty Shades of Grey is coming out next week.
  《五十度灰》下周上映。

- **beginning** [n] 开始；起点
  I fell in love with her in the beginning.
  我一开始就爱上她了。

Daily Sentences 高频用句 | 一分钟学一句，不怕不够用 MP3 10-05

- Can we reserve the movie tickets online?
  我们可以在网上订购电影票吗？

- I like **horror movies** *1.
  我喜欢恐怖片。

- The movies are rated in 5 groups. They are G (general audience), PG (parental **guidance** suggested), PG-13 (under 13 parents strongly **cautioned**), R (restricted-under 17 requires parents or adult **accompanying**) and, NC-17 (no one 17 or under 17 suggested).
  电影被分为五级，它们是普级、辅导级、13岁以下的辅导级、17岁以下需由成人陪同的限制级，以及17岁以下的限制级。

- What kind of movies do you like?
  你喜欢哪种电影？

- You can go to the website for the movie theater and reserve the seats and the tickets online.
  你可以去这个电影院的网址，然后在网上预订你的座位和票就可以了。

- What movie genres do you know?
  你知道的电影种类有哪些？

- Which room is *Harry Potter 3* playing in?
  《哈利·波特3》在哪个厅播放？

- Do you have any **promotional** tickets?
  你有公关票吗？

- Who is in the movie?
  电影里有哪些明星？

★ 换个单词说说看 | 用单词丰富句子，让句子更漂亮！

horror movies *1 可替换：

| romance 浪漫爱情片 | comedy 喜剧 | action movie 动作片 | I like _____. 我喜欢_____。 |

Additional Vocabulary & Phrases | 补充单词 & 短语

- guidance [n] 指导、引导
  I need your guidance.
  我需要你指导。

- caution [n] 小心、谨慎
  Mom always drives with caution.
  妈妈开车总是很小心。

- accompany [v] 陪同、陪随
  She always accompanies me whenever I need her.
  每当我需要她的时候她都陪着我。

- promotional [a] 增进的、促销的
  They have a promotional sale.
  他们有一个促销特卖。

Daily Vocabulary 语言学校都会教的实用日常单词

① film genre 电影种类

comedy	[ˈkɒmədi] n	喜剧
tragedy	[ˈtrædʒədi] n	悲剧
romantic movie	ph	爱情片
action movie	ph	动作片
horror movie	ph	恐怖片
sitcom	[ˈsɪtkɒm] n	情景喜剧
soap opera	ph	肥皂剧

② food bar 食物吧

popcorn	[ˈpɒpkɔːn] n	爆米花
pop	[pɒp] n	汽水
churros	n	西班牙油条
sundae	[ˈsʌndeɪ] n	圣代
hot chocolate	ph	热可可
cinnamon bun	ph	肉桂卷

③ seat 座位

audience	[ˈɔːdiəns] n	观众	projector	[prəˈdʒektə] n	投影机
curtain	[ˈkɜːtn] n	幕布	cinema	[ˈsɪnəmə] n	电影院
screen	[skriːn] n	银幕	theater	[ˈθɪətə] n	电影院

4 notice 公告、通知

trailer ['treɪlə] [n] 预告片
advertise ['ædvətaɪz] [v] 为……宣传
announce [ə'naʊns] [v] 宣布
intellectual property rights [ph] 智力财产权
copy ['kɒpi] [v] 拷贝
sponsor ['spɒnsə] [n] 赞助商

5 festival 戏剧节、音乐节

film [fɪlm] [n] 电影
program ['prəʊgræm] [n] 节目
competition [ˌkɒmpə'tɪʃn] [n] 角逐、竞赛
topic ['tɒpɪk] [n] 主题

6 award 奖

Oscar [n] 奥斯卡
red carpet [ph] 红毯
celebrity [sə'lebrəti] [n] 明星
trophy ['trəʊfi] [n] 奖杯
critic ['krɪtɪk] [n] 评论

7 award category 奖项分类

best picture [ph] 最佳影片
best director [ph] 最佳导演
best actress [ph] 最佳女主角
best actor [ph] 最佳男主角
best supporting actress / actor [ph] 最佳女/男配角
best screenplay [ph] 最佳原创剧本
best adapted screenplay [ph] 最佳改编剧本
best film editing [ph] 最佳剪辑
best visual effects [ph] 最佳视觉效果
best sound mixing [ph] 最佳音效
best foreign feature [ph] 最佳外语片

8 staff 工作人员

director [dəˈrektə] [n] 导演
assistant [əˈsɪstənt] [n] 助理
camera operator [ph] 摄影师
make-up artist [ph] 化妆师
modeling artist [ph] 造型师
hair stylist [ph] 发型设计师

Daily Q&A

[会话一]

Q▶ What movies are on screen right now?
现在哪部电影正在上映中？

A▶ They are listed and introduced in the theater brochure.
电影院制作的小册子里都有介绍。

[会话二]

Q▶ Has the movie *Harry Potter 5*, come out yet?
《哈利・波特 5》上映了吗？

A▶ Not yet. It will come out on September 28th.
还没有，它9月28日才上映。

[会话三]

Q▶ Are we allowed to bring our food to the theater?
我们可以带食物到电影院里吗？

A▶ Nope.
不可以。

Proverbs & Idioms 地道谚语与惯用语 | 让句子锦上添花

snuff movie 关于谋杀血腥的电影
I really don't like snuff movies. The murders in the movies are always bloody, cruel and very violent.
我真的不喜欢有关谋杀、血腥的电影。在电影里，谋杀的人总是非常血腥残酷，而且非常暴力。

silver screen 银幕
All the stars of the silver screen are here tonight to celebrate the New Year.
电影里的所有明星，今晚都聚在这里庆祝新年。

award someone something 颁奖某人某物
The company awarded the employees prizes for full attendance in one month.
这个公司给一个月都没请假的员工颁发全勤奖。

movie genre 电影种类
The movie genres include horror, sci-fi, romantic, comedy, tragedy and so on.
电影的种类包含恐怖片、科幻片、浪漫片、喜剧、悲剧等。

movie review 电影影评
The movie review of this movie says "It is a movie you can't miss once in your life time."
这部电影的影评说："这是一部你一生不能错过的电影。"

film over 蒙上一层薄膜
The windows had filmed over because of all the humidity.
窗户因为湿气已经蒙上了一层薄膜。

double feature 双片放映的电影
Rocky Horror Film is a double feature movie. It consists of two stories.
《洛基恐怖秀》是一部双片放映的电影。它是由两个故事组成的。

spook somebody out 惊吓某人
That horror movie really spooked me out.
那部恐怖片真的吓到我了。

killer 很厉害或很棒的事
The concert was a killer.
那演唱会棒极了。

Unit 38 Go to a KTV 唱 KTV

Daily Conversation 日常对话 | 模拟真实的日常对话

A Wow! The song books are like dictionaries. Let me check whether they have Jolin's new song.
哇！这些歌本就像字典一样，让我查查里面是不是有蔡依林的那首新歌。

B Look at the front page. The newly released songs are usually listed on the first page.
看一下第一页，新发行的歌通常都会被列在第一页。

A Yes! It's there. Let me key in the number of this song. My voice is low. How can I adjust the pitch?
是的，在那里！让我把歌曲号编输入进去。我的声音很低，我要怎么调整音调呢？

B You can use the remote control. Can you see the buttons for low and high keys?
你可以用遥控器。你看到了调音调高低的按钮吗？

A Yes. If I want to turn up the key, do I press the high key and vice versa?
是的。如果我要调高音调，我就按"高音调"的按钮吗？低音调也是吗？

B Absolutely!
对！

Additional Vocabulary & Phrases | 补充单词 & 短语

- **front** [n] 前面、正面
Please write your name on the front.
请在前面写下你的名字。

- **release** [v] 释放、解放
He released the dog.
他把狗放了。

- **adjust** [v] 调整、适应
I cannot adjust the life in India.
我无法适应在印度的生活。

- **absolutely** [ad] 绝对地、完全地
It's absolutely none of your business.
这件事情与你一点关系也没有。

Daily Sentences 高频用句 | 一分钟学一句，不怕不够用

- How can I search for the songs into the song book?
  我要怎样在歌本里找到这些歌呢？

- You can search for them by using the number of the words in the name of the song.
  你可以用歌名的字数来找。

- Can we reserve a room for 15 people?
  我们可以预约一个 15 人的包厢吗？

- We have one more friend is coming. Can we leave a message in the guestbook?
  我们还有一个朋友会来。我们可以在访客留言本上留言吗？

- Do you accept credit cards[1]?
  你们接受信用卡吗？

- Are we required to pay a minimum charge?
  我们有基本消费吗？

- If you need anything in the room at a KTV, you can press the button to ask for service.
  如果你在 KTV 的包厢里需要什么东西的话，只要按服务铃就可以了。

- Is there a restroom in the room or do we have to use the one in the hallway?
  包厢里有厕所吗？还是我们得用走道上的那一个？

- What songs do you want to sing then? Tell me the number and I can key it in for you.
  你想唱的歌是哪些呢？告诉我号码，我可以帮你输入。

★ 换个单词说说看 | 用单词丰富句子，让句子更漂亮！

credit cards[1] 可以替换：

debit card	check	cash	Do you accept _____?
现金卡	支票	现金	你们收_____吗？

Additional Vocabulary & Phrases | 补充单词 & 短语

- **reserve** [v] 预约、预订
  I have reserved a table at the restaurant.
  我在餐厅预订了一桌。

- **guestbook** [n] 来宾签名本、访客留言本
  We need to prepare a guestbook for her wedding.
  我们需要在她的婚礼上准备一本来宾签名本。

- **require** [v] 需要
  The professor requires us to write an essay.
  教授要求我们写一篇小论文。

- **hallway** [n] 走廊
  They kissed at the hallway.
  他们在走廊上相吻。

Daily Vocabulary 语言学校都会教的实用日常单词

1 service 服务

reservation	[ˌrezə'veɪʃn] [n]	预订
option	['ɒpʃn] [n]	选择
consume	[kən'sjuːm] [v]	消费
clean	[kliːn] [v]	清洁
reserved room	[ph]	包厢
assign	[ə'saɪn] [v]	指定

2 sing 唱歌

request a song	[ph]	点歌
cancel	['kænsl] [v]	取消
insert	[ɪn'sɜːt] [v]	插入
function	['fʌŋkʃn] [n]	功能
karaoke	[ˌkæri'əʊki] [n]	卡拉 OK
songbook	['sɒŋbʊk] [n]	歌本
voice activation	[ph]	声控

3 facility 设备

microphone	['maɪkrəfəʊn] [n]	麦克风	cocktail	['kɒkteɪl] [n]	鸡尾酒
disco ball	[ph]		迪斯科球灯	groove	[gruːv] [v]	尽情享受
flirt	[flɜːt] [v]	搭讪	music video	[ph]	音乐录影带

4 purpose 目的

pastime ['pɑːstaɪm] n	消遣、娱乐	contest ['kɒntest] n	比赛
party ['pɑːti] n	聚会、派对	practice ['præktɪs] n v	练习

5 song 歌曲

- **singer** ['sɪŋə] n ······ 歌手
- **composer** [kəm'pəʊzə] n ······ 作曲家
- **lyricist** ['lɪrɪsɪst] n ······ 词作者
- **critic** ['krɪtɪk] n ······ 评论家

6 tone 音调

- **pitch** [pɪtʃ] n ······ 音高
- **tune** [tjuːn] n ······ 旋律、准确的音调
- **high** [haɪ] a ······ 高音调的
- **low** [ləʊ] a ······ 低音的
- **voice** [vɔɪs] n ······ 声音

7 types of music 音乐种类

K-pop [n] .... 韩国流行音乐
J-pop [n] .... 日本流行音乐
blues [bluːz] [n] .... 蓝调
rap [ræp] [n] .... 说唱系
jazz [dʒæz] [n] .... 爵士
electronic [ɪˌlekˈtrɒnɪk] [n] ... 电子

8 music awards 音乐奖项

Grammy Awards [ph] .... 格莱美音乐奖
World Music Awards [ph] ... 世界音乐奖
American Music Awards [ph] .. 全美音乐奖
MTV Europe Music Awards [ph] .. 欧洲音乐大奖
Golden Melody Awards [ph] .. 金曲奖

Daily Q&A

〔会话一〕
Q▶ What's your pastime activity?
你的休闲活动是什么？
A▶ I like to sing at the KTV.
我喜欢在 KTV 唱歌。

〔会话二〕
Q▶ Let's have a singing contest!
我们来唱歌比赛吧！
A▶ Why not!
好啊！

〔会话三〕
Q▶ How often do you go to KTV?
你多久去一次 KTV？
A▶ I go there twice a month.
我一个月去两次。

Proverbs & Idioms 地道谚语与惯用语 | 让句子锦上添花

sell something for a song 以便宜的价格出售
The man had to sell his house for a song because he needed money in a hurry.
那个男人因为急需用钱以低价出售了自己的房子。

swan song 过世与退休前最后一个表演作品
The actress is going to retire soon. The show last night was her swan song.
那个女演员即将退休，昨天晚上是她的告别演出。

set the tone 奠定基调
He was very angry at her lateness for the party yesterday evening, and that also set the tone for the whole evening.
他对她昨天晚上在派对上迟到很生气，那破坏了整个晚上的气氛。

lower the tone 降低标准、格调
Please do not tell rude jokes. It is certain to lower the tone of the whole evening.
不要讲低级的笑话，那一定会降低整个夜晚的格调。

out of tune 走调、不协调
Your idea is out of tune with my idea of what we are supposed to be doing.
你的点子和我们最初想做的完全不一样。

lay low and sing small 低调行事
Jack is looking for you, and he sure was angry. You'd better lay low and sing small.
杰克到处找你，当然他很生气。你最好做事低调一点。

sing for someone's supper 帮某人做事以换取食物做报酬
Howard's upstairs fixing my computer. I'm making him sing for his supper.
霍华德在楼上帮我修东西。我等下会请他吃东西。

sing the blues 抱怨
Many graduates are singing the blues because economy is bad and it is hard to find a good job.
很多毕业生抱怨因为经济不好找不到好工作。

Everyday Sentences 语言学校独家传授的必备好句子

- We are planning to have a class reunion next week. Any suggestions?
  我们下星期要举办班级聚会。有什么建议吗？

- Jolin's new song just came out last week. I want to practice singing it before our reunion and show it in our reunion.
  蔡依林的新歌上周才刚出来，我想在我们聚会前先练唱，然后在聚会的时候秀给大家听。

- We can go to Hollyday KTV. They are having special offers for students.
  我们可以去 Hollday KTV。他们给学生特别的优惠。

- I am Jim Chen. We reserved a room for two.
  我是陈吉姆。我预约了一个两人的包厢。

- Welcome to Hollyday KTV! Did you make your reservation?
  欢迎来到 Hollyday KTV，你们预约了吗？

- Wow! This KTV is so big and beautiful.
  哇！这间 KTV 真的又大又漂亮！

- Let me check my list. Your box is room 534. It's on the 5th floor.
  让我看看我的名单。是的，你们的包厢是 534 号，在 5 楼。

- This KTV has a reputation for its song books. They include all kinds of songs. You never need to worry about not being able to find the songs you want.
  这家 KTV 的歌本是出了名的。它包含了各式各样的歌曲，你永远不用担心找不到你要唱的歌。

- Did the song just came out one week ago?
  这首歌是一星期前才发行的吗？

- You can order some drinks when we are in the box.
  我们到包厢的时候可以点些饮料。

- The music of your song is on TV now. You should get ready to show your voice.
  你的歌已经出现在电视上了。你可以准备一展歌喉了。

MEMO

英美国语言学校都在教的 英语会话课

From AM-PM 从早到晚都用得到的必备好句子

- It's time to eat!
  吃饭了！

- I would like to have beef noodles for dinner.
  我晚餐想吃牛肉面。

- You have to eat everything.
  你必须全部吃光。

- Beef is very nutritious.
  牛肉很有营养。

- You have to eat more.
  你必须多吃一点。

- These French fries are stale.
  这些薯条都不新鲜。

- This pizza is greasy.
  这比萨很油腻。

- How many pieces of fried chicken do you want?
  您想要几块炸鸡？

- I can only eat three pieces of pizza.
  我只想吃三块比萨。

- What kind of soft drink do you want?
  你想喝什么饮料？

- Are you sure you grilled the meat long enough?
  你确定你的肉烤得够久吗？

MEMO

- **This meat is really tender.**
  这肉非常嫩。

- **The smoke from the grill keeps blowing on my face.**
  烤肉架的烟一直吹到我脸上。

- **Let's order some vegetables along with the meat.**
  我们点一些蔬菜来搭配肉。

- **What kind of meat is this?**
  这是什么肉？

- **Could you clean the grill for us?**
  你能帮我们清理一下烤肉架吗？

- **I need to buy some mascara.**
  我要买睫毛膏。

- **I like this pink lipstick.**
  我喜欢这支粉色口红。

- **I don't wear make up.**
  我不化妆的。

- **I don't think you need to wear make up.**
  我认为你不需要化妆。

- **Where is the cosmetics section?**
  化妆品区在哪边？

- **Could you show me how to apply this make up?**
  你能示范给我看这化妆品要如何涂抹吗？

MEMO

- The quality of this product isn't good!
  这东西的品质没有那么好。

- I would like to pay by credit card.
  我要用信用卡付款。

- It's time to turn off the TV.
  是关电视的时候了。

- There's no more hot water for a bath.
  没有热水洗澡了。

- I think I'll go to bed now.
  我想我得去睡觉了。

- I'm going to sleep early tonight.
  我今晚要早点睡。

- What do you think of these boots?
  你觉得这些靴子怎么样呢？

- I have too many pairs of shoes at home.
  我家里有太多鞋子了。

- Why don't you try them on?
  你怎么不试穿一下呢？

- What's your budget for the present?
  你买礼物的预算是多少？

- Could you take the price tag off for me?
  能请你帮我把价格标签拿掉吗？

MEMO

- Don't put too much food in the hot pot.
  不要放太多食材到火锅里。

- Do you want to eat Japanese or Korean BBQ?
  你想吃日式还是韩式烤肉?

- I know a good all-you-can-eat BBQ restaurant near my house.
  我知道我家附近有一家不错的可以吃到饱的烧烤店。

- Oh no! I forgot to do my homework!
  哦,不!我忘记做功课了!

- Can I borrow a pencil?
  我能借支铅笔吗?

- Don't sit there and daydream.
  别再坐在那做白日梦了。

- What chapter are we on?
  现在在学第几章?

- What class do we have next?
  我们下一堂是什么课?

- Do you feel like eating some Chinese food?
  你想吃中式料理吗?

- I love Indian food.
  我喜欢印度料理。

- Do you have any lunch specials?
  你们有任何午餐特餐吗?

MEMO

- We're ready to order.
  我们准备好点餐了。

- It's time for coffee break.
  休息时间到了。

- There's a coffee shop around the corner. Let's go!
  转角那边有一家咖啡馆。我们走吧！

- How was work?
  今天工作还好吗？

- I have no idea what to cook for dinner.
  我不知道晚餐要煮什么？

- What's for dinner?
  今天晚上吃什么？

- We're having fried rice for dinner.
  我们晚上吃炒饭。

- Dinner will be ready in ten minutes.
  再有十分钟晚餐就好了。

- I'll have a medium-sized Coke.
  我要中杯可乐。

- The kid's meal comes with a toy.
  儿童餐附有玩具。

- Can I have a pack of ketchup for my fries?
  可以给我一包番茄酱配薯条吗？

MEMO

- Would you like to upgrade your drink and fries?
  您想升级饮料和薯条吗?

- Dipping your meat and vegetables in this sauce will make them taste better.
  把你的肉和菜蘸一点这些酱会更好吃。

- Be careful not to burn yourself.
  小心不要烫到。

- I don't like the taste of chicken.
  我不喜欢鸡肉的味道。

- Make sure you grill the meat thoroughly.
  你确定将肉烤熟了。

- This meat doesn't look very fresh.
  这肉看起来不太新鲜。

- We're having a BBQ on our rooftop tonight.
  我们今天晚上要在屋顶烤肉。

- Could we get some meat with less fat?
  我们可以点一些脂肪比较少的肉吗?

- Be careful not to burn the meat.
  小心不要把肉烤焦了。

- Thanks for taking me out for dinner.
  谢谢你带我出来吃晚餐。

- Please help me clean the table.
  请帮我清桌子。

MEMO

- I'm stuffed!
  我好饱!

- This is not what I ordered.
  这不是我点的食物。

- Could you please pass me the salt and pepper?
  麻烦你把盐和胡椒递给我好吗?

- The food here tastes excellent.
  这里的食物真好吃。

- Would you like some cream and sugar in your coffee?
  您的咖啡要加奶油和糖吗?

- Wash your hands before you eat.
  吃饭前先洗手。

- I made your favorite dish.
  我做了你最爱吃的菜。

- Could you set the table, please?
  你能帮忙放碗筷吗?

- There's more rice in the cooker if you're still hungry.
  如果你还没吃饱,锅里还有饭。

- Could you please hurry up in the bathroom?
  你用厕所能不能快一点啊?

- I can't find my shoes.
  我找不到我的鞋。

MEMO

- It doesn't take me very long to get ready in the morning.
  我早上准备不用太多时间。

- Taking a shower helps me wake up.
  冲个澡可以让我清醒一点。

- Could you brew some coffee for me?
  你能帮我煮些咖啡吗？

- I don't feel like eating anything this morning.
  今天早上我不太想吃东西。

- Do we have any butter for the toast?
  我们还有奶油抹吐司吗？

- I usually skip breakfast in the morning.
  我通常早上不吃早餐。

- I'm usually not hungry in the morning.
  我通常早上不饿。

- Take off your pajamas.
  把睡衣脱掉。

- Put on your coat.
  穿上你的外套。

- Put on your pants.
  穿上你的裤子。

- I hate sitting in traffic.
  我讨厌被困在车阵中。

MEMO

版权专有 侵权必究

图书在版编目（CIP）数据

英美国语言学校都在教的英语会话课 / 黄文俞著.—北京：北京理工大学出版社，2019.7
ISBN 978-7-5682-7229-2

Ⅰ.①英… Ⅱ.①黄… Ⅲ.①英语—口语—自学参考资料 Ⅳ.①H319.9

中国版本图书馆CIP数据核字（2019）第134998号

北京市版权局著作权合同登记号图字：01-2017-2407
简体中文版由我识出版社有限公司授权出版发行
英美国语言学校都在教的英语会话课，Amy黄文俞著，2015年，初版
ISBN：9789864070152

出版发行 / 北京理工大学出版社有限责任公司	
社　　址 / 北京市海淀区中关村南大街5号	
邮　　编 / 100081	
电　　话 / （010）68914775（总编室）	
（010）82562903（教材售后服务热线）	
（010）68948351（其他图书服务热线）	
网　　址 / http://www.bitpress.com.cn	
经　　销 / 全国各地新华书店	
印　　刷 / 天津久佳雅创印刷有限公司	
开　　本 / 710毫米×1000毫米　1/16	
印　　张 / 17.75	责任编辑 / 王俊洁
字　　数 / 549千字	文案编辑 / 王俊洁
版　　次 / 2019年7月第1版　2019年7月第1次印刷	责任校对 / 周瑞红
定　　价 / 78.00元	责任印制 / 李志强

图书出现印装质量问题，请拨打售后服务热线，本社负责调换